HOW TO BE CLEVER

KT-161-881

HELEN GREATHEAD
ILLUSTRATED BY DAVID SEMPLE

SCHOLASTIC

Thanks to Andrew Beasley, Susie Hodge, Bertie McCubbine and others...

Scholastic Children's Books,
Euston House, 24 Eversholt Street,
London NW1 1DB, UK

A division of Scholastic Ltd
London ~ New York ~ Toronto ~ Sydney ~ Auckland
Mexico City ~ New Delhi ~ Hong Kong

Published in the UK by Scholastic Ltd, 2012

Text copyright © Helen Greathead, 2012
Illustration copyright © David Semple, 2012
All rights reserved

ISBN 978 1407 13144 3

Printed and bound by CPI Group (UK) Ltd, Croydon, CRO 4YY

2 4 6 8 10 9 7 5 3 1

The right of Helen Greathead and David Semple to be identified as the author and illustrator of this work respectively has been asserted by them in accordance with the Copyright, Designs and Patents Act, 1988.

This book is sold subject to the condition that it shall not, by way of trade or otherwise be lent, resold, hired out, or otherwise circulated without the publisher's prior consent in any form or binding other than that in which it is published and without a similar condition, including this condition, being imposed upon the subsequent purchaser.

Papers used by Scholastic Children's Books are made from woods grown in sustainable forests.

CONTENTS

TIME TO GET CLEVER

Are there parts of your brain that might benefit from a little more exercise? Do you ever wish you were better at asking questions in class? Is your homework just good when it could be amazing?

It's okay, you can be honest — no one's going to tell you off here. In fact, you're just the sort of reader this book needs ... the sort who might like a little help to realize your true brilliance.

This book includes tips, short cuts and memory tricks that will help you to boost your very valuable brainpower. It will show you how to play a tune, appreciate art and conduct a proper science experiment.

Want to know...
- How having a good snooze or doodling in lessons can actually help your brain?
- How some famous geniuses got on at school?
- Why you shouldn't bother with intelligence tests?

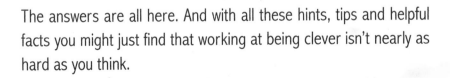

The answers are all here. And with all these hints, tips and helpful facts you might just find that working at being clever isn't nearly as hard as you think.

WHAT TYPE OF CLEVER ARE YOU?

Experts always seem to be arguing with each other. And one thing the experts of 'clever' can't agree on is just what intelligence *is* exactly. Some say that there are several different types of intelligence (though they argue about the exact number). If you'd like to have a go at finding out what type of clever you are, here's one quick way to find out. See if you can recognize yourself among any of these characters.

Type: Mover
How to spot: They like hanging out in a tracksuit, football kit, leotard or tutu, and they never stop moving. Outside class, they'll be bouncing a ball, balancing on their tippy toes, or charging around the playing field. Even in class they're always looking for an excuse to jump up from the desk, and jiggle their legs up and down

when they can't think of one. Movers are often very hands on too, so they probably make the best paper aeroplanes, pea shooters and life-sized, 3D, papier mâché models of the teacher.

What they say: "Fancy a kickaround?" or, "I can do the splits."

Jobs they do: Anything to do with sport – dancer, fitness instructor, Premier League Footballer...

Type: Friendly

How to spot: They're the ones with the big beaming smile being followed around at break by a group of adoring fans. They're great at making friends, and never short of something to say. But they can be caring too. When two mates fall out over who pushed who in the dinner queue, it's Friendly who sorts them out. And when you have to do teamwork in class, nobody minds if Friendly takes the lead.

What they say: "I'd love to come to your party, thanks." or, "How are you feeling today?"

Jobs they do: Anything connected with people – receptionist, teacher, sales person, counsellor, prime minister...

Type: Dreamer

How to spot: In class, they're usually gazing out of the window. They don't cause trouble, but when the teacher asks them a question they often haven't a clue what's going on. Dreamers like to decorate things: exercise books, their pencil case, the bedroom, themselves. They're into all things visual and like learning through pictures best: paintings, photographs, even maps will grab their attention.

What they say: "I'm sorry, did you say something?"

Jobs they do: Sign writer, graphic/interior designer, painter, sculptor, architect — especially if they've got Logic too (see p. 11), fashion guru.

Type: Thinker

How to spot: Thinkers like to keep themselves in the background, so they can be hard to spot. They might be in the corner on their own, or whispering to no more than a couple of friends. Thinkers don't gossip in the toilets — they speak when they've got something to say, and that might not be all that often. There's plenty going on in their heads though, and they know themselves pretty well. They take their time working out problems, but they're great at coming up with answers ... eventually.

What they say: "Erm,........"

Jobs they do: They are excellent at academic study, and might do well in psychology or philosophy — finding out the thoughts of Thinkers from the past.

Type: Muso

How to spot: They might be humming (in tune) quietly to themselves, or plugged into their iPod, head nodding in time to the beat. In class they can be annoying, always tapping out rhythms on the desk with a pen. Muso's exercise books are covered with stickers of their favourite bands. They might even play an instrument or two. One way or another, they like to fill their world with the sound of music.

What they say: "You've got to listen to this. Flaming Pencil are going to be MEGA!"

Jobs they do: They might produce music, put on gigs, become a music teacher, set up a retro vinyl shop ... or sing solo in front of squillions of people in the O_2 Arena.

Type: Bookworm

How to spot: They're into puns, jokes, poems and maybe even write their own. They almost certainly keep a diary. In class they've probably got their nose in a book, and scoot quickly to the dictionary if they come across a word they don't know. They'll always let the teacher know if she's misspelled something on the board, because, for Bookworm, words are where it's at.

What they say: "Remember 'i' before 'e' except after 'c.'"

Jobs they do: English teacher, editor, journalist, poet, author of a multi-million-selling series of books for children.

Type: Mr or Ms Logic

How to spot: They've always got their hands up in science and maths classes. They like getting into discussions with the teacher, and they're quick to solve problems by breaking them down into manageable chunks. They think numbers are fun and are annoyingly good at looking after their pocket money. Then, when they've saved up enough to buy whatever it is they want — a fancy new calculator, maybe — they don't get lost on their way to the shop, because, guess what? They have a great sense of direction too!

What they say: "$E = mc^2$? What do you mean you don't get it?"
Jobs they do: Anything that involves numbers. Accountant, maths/science teacher, scientist, Governor of the Bank of England.

Did you recognize yourself among any of those characters? You might not fit one group exactly. We probably all have a little of each type, but the two or three that sound most like you are your 'dominant intelligence'.

WAYS TO SEEM CLEVER

How do you react when a teacher asks you a question that really puts you on the spot? If you don't know the answer straightaway, do you panic, shrug and blurt out nonesense in a panic?

If you answered "yes" to that question, then these tips should be really helpful.

First of all, you don't have to answer the question quickly. Relax, take your time, have a think. It might just be that you need a bit of time to remember the answer. If you don't know, don't worry — ask yourself how to work it out, or if you can think of any information to help you? While you're thinking, make sure you're not giving your best impression of a frightened rabbit.

13

Don't say, "Er," say, "Well ..." and try to look relaxed, thoughtful – clever even. Then answer calmly – you could even use a paper and pen to help you. You might not be able to work out the answer every time, but there are plenty of ways to get out of having to say, "I don't know." You could try:

- "I'm sorry, could you repeat the question please?"
- "I'm sure I know this – I just need some time to think about it."
- "It's an interesting question, but I'm not sure I know the answer."

Just letting your teacher know you are thinking about the question is going to make you look that little bit cleverer.

Even if you can't work out the answer, you can use little bits of information that pop into your brain to help you:

Teacher: "Where in the world we would find Caracas ... Eliot?"

Eliot: (panicking inwardly, but cucumber cool on the outside) "I'm not absolutely certain. The name sounds Spanish, but I don't think Caracas is in Spain. Is it somewhere in South America?"

Teacher: "Well done, Eliot, you're right! Now, can anyone else tell me which country in South America we're talking about?"

This way you can get praise without even answering the question. In fact, you've just done something that's particularly clever: you've answered one question with another question. By the way, in case you didn't already know, Caracas is in Venezuela.

Why asking questions is clever

Asking good questions is a clear sign of intelligence. According to one statistic, teachers ask 300 to 400 questions a day. And teachers like pupils who ask questions, too. It shows they're:

- Paying attention
- Interested in the lesson
- Still awake.

So, if a whole lesson is going way over your head, don't just sit there worrying. Chances are if you can't understand what the teacher is saying, others in your class are having the same trouble. Put your hand up and say, "I'm really sorry, I'm afraid you've lost me. Would you mind explaining that again?"

To ask the cleverest questions, you need to be able to listen, and that isn't as easy as it sounds. Most of us only remember between 25% and 50% of what we're told. There are so many distractions. But, if you can push from your mind all thoughts about ...

- What everyone else in the class is doing
- What's for tea
- How to beat your best score in Angry Hamsters

... you'll find you are free to concentrate.

Next, look at your teacher, focus on them and really take in what they are saying. You might find that lessons are suddenly a bit more interesting, that you can understand them loads better, and there's a chance questions will just pop into your head.

And by the way, it's not just your teacher you need to listen to. Listen to yourself too (once you've got rid of all those distractions). What's that niggling at the back of your mind? Could it be a question? Quick, don't be scared, pop your hand up and ask. Be bold, give it a go, you might be surprised by the result.

Famously clever: Socrates (469-399 BC)

Where would we be today if nobody ever asked any questions? Living in a cave draped in bearskins, that's where.

All progress happened because people started asking questions. Why can't I fly? What made that apple fall on my head? How can we be sure that the earth is flat?

Socrates was an ancient Greek thinker, or philosopher, who lived over 2,000 years ago. He believed that people learned better through discussing things. Socrates asked lots of questions and encouraged everyone else to do the same. We don't know much about him because he didn't write anything down, but one of his students – another famous philosopher called Plato – did and that's how we know a few bits and pieces about Socrates.

Although Socrates had plenty of fans and followers, he still managed to get himself sentenced to death because the rulers of the time didn't like that he was asking lots of questions. They said it defied the Gods. But if the Greeks thought killing Socrates was going to kill off his philosophy, they were badly mistaken: his way of thinking and questioning – or 'critical thinking', as it is known – is still used today.

Can puzzles make you clever?

Did you know that there are machines and computer games designed just to help train and improve your brain? The machines are fine, but scientists say that you can do your brain just as much good (and save yourself a lot of money) with a crossword in a newspaper.

How crosswords saved the world

During the Second World War, the Secret Service was on the lookout for cryptic crossword addicts. The Daily Telegraph newspaper even set a particularly fiendish crossword in order to seek out some top-notch puzzlers.

If you could solve their puzzle in less than 12 minutes, you were invited to Military Intelligence offices for another test. If you passed that one, you were asked to pack your bags, head for a small town north of London, and tell no one where you were going.

The town was Bletchley, in Buckinghamshire, and your destination was a stately home, called Bletchley Park. Here you'd be joining Britain's most brilliant professors and students of maths and languages, chess champions and academic aristocrats, in order to help solve one enormous puzzle.

The puzzle was called Enigma, and it was, in fact, an ingenious machine, put to use by the German navy, to send secret messages to their battleships. It looked a bit like an old-fashioned typewriter, but with wheels at the top that could scramble ordinary (German) words in millions of different ways. It made codes that were impossible to crack – unless you had an identical machine, and knew how to set it up. Without the machine, Enigma was absolutely foolproof. Or so the Germans thought…

They hadn't reckoned on the army of intellectuals working 24/7, to break the codes. With the help of some Polish mathematicians, the invention of a couple of decoding machines, mistakes made by the German message writers, and some clever sideways thinking, the Bletchley residents really did crack the Enigma code.

Some historians reckon that the code-breaking at Bletchley Park helped shorten the war by up to four years! That's some impressive work by clever crossword solvers.

Are you clever enough to code crack?

Enigma messages looked a bit like this (but much, much longer):

OGG VOG DAV JGV QKN GVU CVP QQP

Before the code-crackers could solve the puzzle, they had to work out what the code was. For this one, the letters of the alphabet have all been moved forwards two places. You can work out the message by using the grid below. The first row shows the normal alphabet — the second row shows the alphabet the message is written in. Find each letter from the message in the second row, replace it with the letter immediately above it in the first row, and you should be able to decode the message:

A B C D E F G H I J K L M N O P Q R S T U V W X Y Z
C D E F G H I J K L M N O P Q R S T U V W X Y Z A B

Does your answer look like this?

MEE TME BYT HET OIL ETS ATN OON

Well done! Oh, wait. It still doesn't make any sense. That'll be because all the spaces are in the wrong place. See if you can work out where they should be.*

*If you got this answer: MEET ME BY THE TOILETS AT NOON — then you've cracked it.

IQ tests

IQ stands for 'Intelligence Quotient'. The tests that have been used for years by employers, armies, schools and colleges to find the cleverest people. But, funnily enough, they were invented for the totally opposite reason.

In the early 1900s, the French government made it compulsory for all children to attend school. In order to find anyone who might need extra help, they asked a psychologist, called Alfred Binet, to devise a test that children could take even if they hadn't started school yet.

Binet did as he was told, though he was convinced true intelligence tests should look at things like where the children came from, not just how well they scored.

Despite his doubts, the tests caught on and, though they've changed over time, they're still in use. However, experts today agree that IQ changes under different circumstances — your score can go up, and it can go down. It's likely to be lower if:

- You have missed a lot of school
- Your birthday is at the end of the school year
- It's the summer holidays (when you're not forced to study all the time!)
- The weather is particularly hot and humid
- You're feeling ill or having a bad day.

The test finds an average score for your age group, and then works out where your score fits in the pecking order. Most of us will achieve between 90 and 109. Over 130 is really clever and 180 is heading off the scale — although the highest ever recorded scores were over 200! A score of 69 or below, on the other hand, probably means a bit of help is needed.

The tests have been through various updates, and if you ever have to take one, just remember that the IQ test will only assess certain areas of your intelligence — and that your score might be different from one day to the next.

Famously clever: Albert Einstein (1879-1955)

Albert Einstein was born in Germany in 1879. His family were anxious about him from quite early on. He looked odd as a baby, and he didn't really start to talk until he was three. He was slow, thoughtful and his speech was still clumsy when he was nine. His parents worried that he was below average intelligence.

Albert's biggest problem was that he didn't like school, but it turned out his maths was amazing and he was great at music. He learned far better by himself at home though — with the help of his maths and science books.

Albert kept on studying hard and, in 1896, he went to the Institute of Technology in Zurich, Switzerland. He still didn't bother to go to class though. He preferred to work by himself in the library, or in a laboratory. It was lucky he had a friend who didn't mind sharing his lecture notes.

Albert graduated with a Physics degree, but failed to get a job as a teacher at a university so he got an office job instead. He carried on studying at night though and, as a result, Albert wrote four papers, which presented some earth-shattering scientific ideas. One of them included the famous maths equation $E = mc^2$, which is about the speed of light. The papers meant Albert got a job at the University of Zurich in Switzerland and no longer had to work in an office.

In 1914, Albert moved back to Germany and started working for the University of Berlin. He kept on working hard and, in 1916, he came up with the famous 'General Theory of Relativity', which redefined the laws of gravity. After all his hard work and successful papers Albert was awarded the Nobel Prize for Physics in 1921.

From here on, Albert became a big celebrity. Almost everything he did made headline news. He travelled the world, got involved in politics, opposed wars and called for one international government.

Estimates put Albert's IQ at between 120 and 150, but the result wouldn't have interested him. He said: "It's not that I'm so smart, I just stay with problems longer." He often had to ask for help in working out the maths for his theories.

Brain Box – Nobel Prizes

The Nobel Prizes were set up after the brilliant and successful scientist, Alfred Nobel, died in 1896. He'd asked that his vast fortune be used to reward achievements in sciences, medicine, literature and for peace. The first prizes were awarded in 1901, and they're still going strong over 100 years later. Other than Einstein, some famous Nobel Prize winners include former US president Theodore Roosevelt for Peace in 1905, scientist Marie Curie for Chemistry in 1911, poet William Yeats for Literature in 1923, equal rights campaigner Martin Luther King Jr for Peace in 1964, and missionary Mother Teresa for Peace in 1979.

Improve your imagination

So what can you do to get a better imagination?

The thing is, you probably already have what it takes. Did you make up your own games when you were little, have an imaginary friend, draw wild pictures or tell ridiculous stories?

When you were small, you were allowed to be imaginative. Everyone thought it was cute. Now you're older, you're told to think this way or that way. But there are loads of great ways to spark your imagination. Try reading a story that really grabs you, looking at interesting pictures, going to a museum, gallery, theatre, or joining after-school clubs.

Why not try these exercises at home to get your imagination flowing:

1. Take a blank sheet of A4 paper, a pen and some sort of timer. Set the timer to three minutes. Now start writing and see if you can keep going until the time is up. Write whatever comes into your head. If you can't think of anything, say so. If you find yourself staring at the wall, write about that. Don't think too hard, just to let your thoughts flow.

If you can get into the habit of doing this regularly, you might be surprised by what comes out of that head of yours!

2. Ask someone to choose a piece of music for you. It's probably best if it doesn't have any words. Then do exactly the same as you did for number 1. Just see what comes into your head and get it down on paper before the end of the music.

3. Keep a notebook beside your bed, and if you wake up remembering an incredible dream, jot it down quickly. Talk about your dreams with your friends, and encourage them to tell you about theirs. The more aware you are of your dreams, the more likely you are to remember them. The more you remember them, the more you can make use of them.

Imagination makes a difference to just about anything you do. You never know when an experience is going to come in handy.

Famously clever: Steve Jobs (1955-2011)

In the 1970s, Steve Jobs was finishing school and not sure what to do with his life. He liked arts subjects – he was a big fan of calligraphy (beautiful handwriting), and an even bigger fan of music. But he liked technology too – he'd learnt about electronics from his dad, and there was plenty of work in computers in California, USA, where Steve lived.

Finally, Steve Jobs decided to have a go at making his own computers in the garage with his friend Steve Wozniak. The computers sold well, and the pair started a company called Apple Macintosh.

Back then, computers were for work and not for fun, but Steve Jobs thought differently. He reckoned ordinary people could use computers and built a computer that could be used straight out of the box. Before this they had to be built by an expert. He wanted the computers to be stylish too – even the boxes they came in looked good – and that's still just as important for the company today.

Over the years, Steve Jobs worked on more ideas and even focused on music, developing the iPod, iTunes store, the iPhone and iPad.

When he died in 2011, aged just 56, he had changed the world by taking ideas from his own experience and imagining a different way forwards. Oh, and he'd become a billionaire, too!

Get a clever memory

Chimps have better memories than humans. It's true! When scientists gave a groups of chimps and humans the same test — to remember the numbers one to nine in different positions on a computer screen — the chimps came out on top every time. It seems their memories are almost photographic. Scientists believe that our human memories were once as good as this, but that over time we have lost some of our memory skills.

Hundreds of years ago, being clever was all about having a good memory. With few books and newspapers, no TVs, Internet or telephones, storytellers and scholars were expected to memorize really long poems and stories. But it wasn't all down to natural ability. The stories often had their own in-built memory tricks such as repetition, rhythm and rhyme. Memory techniques were passed down from generation to generation and those techniques work just as well today.

...lace in your mind

...ncient Greek legend tells how a poet named Simonides of Ceos, was called out of a banqueting hall just before the roof collapsed, killing everyone inside. The bodies were so badly crushed that no one knew who was who.

By thinking about what was in the hall, and who had been talking to whom, Simonides realized he could remember where each guest had been sitting, so the bodies were identified.

The key to memorizing just about anything is to link it to an image that you won't forget, in a place you know really well. It's a technique called a 'Memory Palace'. You can make up your own and this is where a good imagination comes in handy.

Making a Memory Palace

Imagine it's the last day of term, and you have more things than usual to remember to take to school. Your own amazing Memory Palace will make sure you don't forget anything.

1. Choose your palace

Choose a place or journey that's really familiar to you. It could be your house, your granny's house, your school or the route you walk to school – anywhere really.

2. Associate

Now, think of the things you have to remember:

- That Harry Potter library book that's six weeks overdue
- A box of chocolates as a 'thank you' for your teacher
- All the dinner money you've forgotten to pay this term
- Your email address for the holidays to give to your friends
- A jester's hat, for your final assembly
- The *Simpson's* DVD you borrowed and keep forgetting to return.

Then think of an object that you associate with each item on the list, this way you don't have to remember every little detail. The object can be as weird and wonderful as you like because the weirder the association, the more likely the thing is to stick out when you walk around your palace.

3. Place the objects in your palace

Let's use your house as the Memory Palace. We'll start at the front door, with the Harry Potter book. Imagine a wand is attached to the door and it's fizzing and sparking with magical spells. The sparking wand will remind you of magic, which reminds you of Harry Potter and *ta-dah!* in one simple step through your front door you've remembered the Harry Potter book.

Next, you open the door, step into the hall, and find melted chocolate all over the carpet — that's a bit unusual. But the melted chocolate will remind you of the box of chocolates for your teacher, brilliant!

So, you step over the melted chocolate and walk into the sitting room, where a huge, greasy dinner plate has replaced the table, which reminds you of your overdue dinner money.

Now, moving up the stairs your landing has been replaced with a swimming pool. This will remind you to give your email address to you friends, so you can stay in touch over the holidays (it doesn't matter if you're actually going camping and there won't be a pool).

After swimming across the landing you see a red, green and blue jester's hat with bells on dancing in front of the bathroom door — well that's easy enough to remember what it relates to.

Finally, going to the bathroom to dry off, you open the door to find the entire cast of the *Simpsons* in the bath, on the loo and brushing their teeth at the washbasin. You definitely won't forget to take back the DVD now. And that's it — simple!

4. Test your palace

Now see if you can remember the list, without looking. By taking this imaginary walk through your house a few times it's unlikely you'll forget any of it. You can use this route through your palace over and over again to remember all sorts of different things. You can also make the journey around your palace longer or shorter depending on how many things you have to remember. The best bit is once you've learned your route really well, it gets easier each time to walk it and spot different things that you've added.

Memory championships

Did you know that there is a contest called the World Memory Championship? Expert memorizers come from all over the world to test their skills at memorizing:

- The order of the 52 cards in a pack (sometimes several packs)
- Lists of random words
- A poem
- Details (such as telephone numbers and addresses) of people they've never met.

Some of the best contestants can memorize all the images in a pack of cards in just 30 seconds! But they weren't born with this skill — instead they've learned techniques and spent an awful lot of time practising and perfecting them.

After covering the US Memory Championships as a journalist one year, Joshua Foer — who claimed to have a hopeless memory — was set a challenge: to learn memory techniques and practise for at least half an hour every day, and then to enter the US Memory Championship the following year. He did just that, and through a lot of hard work, a whole string of Memory Palaces and a certain amount of luck, he emerged as that year's US Memory Champion!

Teachers don't like doodles...

If you sometimes get into trouble with your teacher for doodling in lessons, here's some good news — tests have shown that doodling actually helps your concentration. You're more likely to remember what you're being taught if you doodle at the same time.

Scientists think this is because doodling doesn't take up too much of your brain, so you can still concentrate on what's being said. But a full-blown daydream where you wander off to foreign parts, lie on a beach slurping fresh melon juice ... demands much more from your brain and distracts you completely from stuff you're supposed to be listening to.

Mind you, some teachers complain that doodlers can get a bit carried away with their doodles and forget to take notes in lessons. Well, you could easily make up for that, by combining your doodles with a Mind Map! (See p. 36.)

...but they don't mind Mind Maps

In school as you get older, you won't get away with not paying attention — you'll be expected to organize yourself more, and take notes on whatever your teacher is explaining.

Note-taking is a bit of a skill. The trick is to not write down everything that's being said — you probably won't be able to write fast enough and you'll end up with a page full of scribble that you can't read. Instead, it's a good idea to work out little abbreviations for words, and use symbols to help you speed up.

If you've ever sent a text, you'll probably know some good abbreviations already. Remember, don't use them for a finished piece of work, but when it comes to note-taking 'text-talk' is gr8! There are other tried and tested symbols that you can use too:

aka = also known as

amap = as much as possible

asap = as soon as possible

b4 = before

& = and

c.f. = compare

etc. = etcetera, and so on

e.g. = for example

= = equals!

≠ = doesn't equal

i.e. = that is

No. or **#** = number

n.b. = note well (for things that are really important)

∵ = because

∴ = however

w/o = without

w/ = with

Of course, you can make up your own abbreviations, too, but the cleverest way to take note of what's being said is by using a Mind Map. These were invented by a man called Tony Buzan, who's written loads of books about how to improve your memory. The idea is that if you can put down everything you need to know or remember on one sheet of paper, it's easier to look at your notes and you don't have to look through pages and pages of scribble.

At first it might be hard to draw up a Mind Map while your teacher is talking, so you could start by taking notes, using abbreviations, and then, while everything from the lesson is still fresh in your mind, turn it into a Mind Map. Let's say you've just had a history lesson on the First World War — here's how you'd draw a Mind Map:

1. Start with a blank sheet of paper, and write the title of your topic in the middle.

2. Draw a circle around the title, and then draw lines coming off it for different areas of the subject that are important, a bit like using headings in your writing.

3. Add more detail by drawing, colouring, shading your Mind Map — whatever will help you to record things quickly and remember them easily when you look back at it.

When you've finished, it should look something like this:

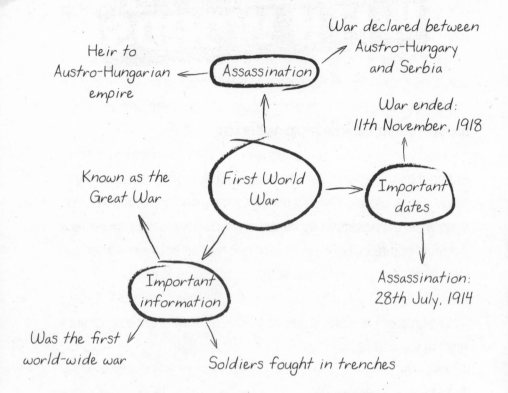

Heir to Austro-Hungarian empire

Assassination

War declared between Austro-Hungary and Serbia

War ended: 11th November, 1918

Known as the Great War

First World War

Important dates

Important information

Assassination: 28th July, 1914

Was the first world-wide war

Soldiers fought in trenches

Mind Maps aren't just for note-taking either, you can use them to help solve a problem (say you want to persuade your parents to let you have eight friends for a sleepover), or organize your thoughts, for example, when you want to write a story (see p. 69). When exams or tests are looming, use your old Mind Maps to help you revise, and then draw up a new one to work out when and how to do your revision.

BE CLEVER WITH WORDS

How to do joined-up writing

If you'd been at school 100 years ago, handwriting would have been just about your most important subject. You would have spent ages trying to achieve beautiful handwriting. And if your hand produced a loopy scribble instead, its knuckles would have been rapped with the teacher's ruler – *ouch!*

Today, even though you can use a computer for most things, handwriting is still really important. If you're at secondary school you'll have to make notes and take tests, write essays, write up experiments, and sit exams. And you'll be expected to do most of these things by hand.

You will need to write

- Fast, to keep up with some teachers
- Neatly, so you can understand your own work
- Clearly, so your teacher (and friends who need to borrow your notes because yours are so much better than theirs) can understand what you're saying.

Quite a lot of clever people find handwriting particularly tricky – but the clever thing is, with a bit of practice, you can get really good at joined-up writing, and you'll find you can take notes and finish homework loads faster. Here's how:

Do you remember learning to write from a load of letters that looked like this?

Remember those tags you learned when you first started writing out the alphabet? They were there, of course, to help you join up your letters, but by the time you got to that stage, were you still remembering to use them?

Try using lined paper to revise those tags now, and keep practising them, whenever you can. When you're writing, make sure you're always sitting in a good position.

Now, work on the letters until they're looking pretty neat, with the tags in the right place every time.

Okay? Now your letters are looking good, we can move on to pangrams. What? You know, those sentences that use all the letters of the alphabet. You might have seen this one before:

The quick brown fox jumps over a lazy dog.

And this one:

How quickly daft jumping zebras vex.

Once you've mastered the letters, have a go at writing these sentences (or try making up your own), so that you get plenty of practice at writing and joining up all the letters of the alphabet. Keep practising and soon you really won't have to think about it.

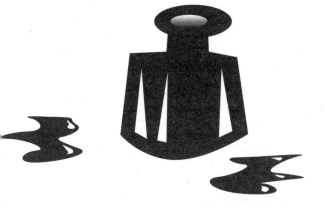

Touch-type

While writing joined up will speed up your note-taking, you will probably still only be able to write 30 words per minute. Typing can be much faster — some people can bash out over 200 words per minute! You don't have to try to go that fast, but learning to touch-type properly can really help you work more speedily.

You can build up speed on a keyboard by making sure you always position your fingers correctly, use both hands and learn which fingers works best on which keys. Trainee typists spend hours practising each letter and each row on the keyboard.

You can try this by assigning a different section of the keyboard to each finger, like this:

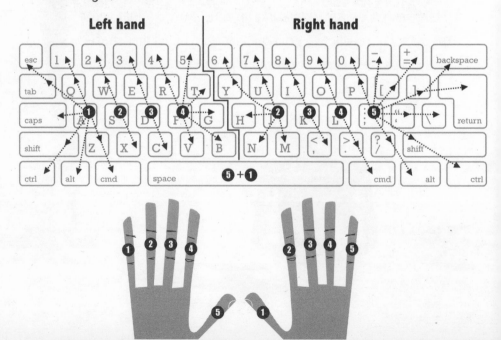

Make sure your left hand only uses the left side of the keyboard and your right hand only uses the right side. If you try to keep your hands in the same position and use all ten of your fingers then you'll find the more you use the keyboard with your fingers in position, the faster you can type.

Brain Box – qwerty
The keyboard has been around for almost 150 years. It started out as a typewriter, but in that time, the keyboard has hardly changed. Funnily enough, the keys were deliberately laid out so that the most common letters were not side by side. This was to stop people typing too fast as the keys would jam together

How well can you spell?

If you're good friends with the spellcheck on your computer, you probably think you don't need to worry much about spellings. But ...

Theres no point haveing supafast handritting, if your speling lets yoo down.

... doesn't look so good, does it?

The English language isn't the easiest one to spell, and that's not surprising when you think that it has 26 letters in its alphabet and many different ways to combine the letters. For example, the innocent looking sound "sh" can be spelt in 13 different ways!

There's a good reason why English spellings are so quirky. Many English words come from other languages and for a long time there was no right or wrong way to spell them.

Brainbox – the dictionary

Dr Samuel Johnson published his *Dictionary of the English Language* in 1755, with definitions for over 40,000 words. It took him nearly nine years to write, and some of the rules it set down are still in use today.

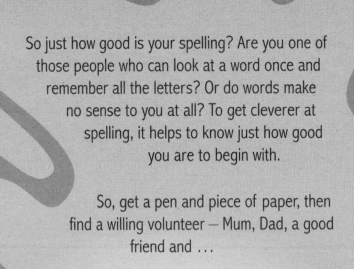

So just how good is your spelling? Are you one of those people who can look at a word once and remember all the letters? Or do words make no sense to you at all? To get cleverer at spelling, it helps to know just how good you are to begin with.

So, get a pen and piece of paper, then find a willing volunteer — Mum, Dad, a good friend and ...

DON'T TURN THE PAGE! Ask your volunteer to look for you and to slowly read out the list of words on page 46, as you have a go at writing them down.

Spelling Test

Volunteers, please read out this list of tricky spellings slowly and clearly without revealing how they are spelt:

beautiful	queue
independent	receive
library	scissors
necessary	separate
occasion	tomorrow
possession	until.

(Now give the book back.)

So how did you get on?

Don't worry too much about your score — these spellings are tough ones. They were picked because they are some of the most misspelled words in the English language. So, if you got ten or more right, wow, well done!

But, if you got a low score, don't worry. The tips on the next few pages will help make sure you never get these spellings wrong EVER again.

Beautiful: Sometimes you can make up a mnemonic, or memory trick, using each letter of the word as an initial. It doesn't have to make complete sense…

Bug Eggs Are Useful To Insects For Unpleasant Lunches

…and a daft thought that will stick in your mind is usually easier to remember.

Independent: It's the vowels that often cause problems in this spelling. Try saying it rhythmically and sounding out the syllables like this:

"In-de-pen-dent has three 'e's"

Library: Use the phrase — "I rarely talk in a library" — to remind you that there's an extra 'r' in this word that doesn't always sound when you say it.

Necessary: Try singing this one along to the tune of *Baa, Baa Black Sheep.*

N	E		C	E		S	S	A-R	Y
Baa	Baa		Black	Sheep		have	you	an-y	wool

If you have trouble remembering whether the third letter is a 'c' or an 's', think about the third word of the song – 'black' – that's got a 'c' in it, but no 's'.

Occasion: People often forget whether this word has two 'c's or two 's's. But, listen carefully – you'll hear that the 's' sound is quite a hard 'zh'. That tells you that there's only one 's', which means the doubled letter must be the 'c'. (Two 's's usually make a softer sound – miss, dismiss, hiss, or, as with possession, a 'sh' sound.)

Possession: Instead of the four 's's imagine four snakes slithering about. They could be hissssing too. If you remember the word has four 's's you're more likely to get this one right.

SSSS

Queue: Just spell out the letters of this word in your head:

q-u-e-u-e

You'll find it has a memorable ring to it.

Receive: Remember the rule, 'i' before 'e', except after 'c'? It works for this spelling, but there are quite a few exceptions.

This version of the rhyme helps with some of those exceptions:

i before e,
Except after c
Or when sounded 'a'
As in neighbour or weigh.

Scissors: Say it in your head as you spell it. Pronounce the hard 'c' and make a long soft 'ss' sound, so you'll remember there are two of them.

Separate: People often misspell this as 'seperate'. Think about "separating two angry parrots" (try to get the image in your head) to remind you that you need an 'a' — because the parrots are angry — and not an 'e'.

Tomorrow: Break this one down into three separate words to remember the two 'r's, 'Tom or row'. Then make a picture in your mind of going to see 'Tom' or 'rowing a boat'.

Until: Confusing, because the word 'till' has two 'l's. So think:

'un'do one 'l'
to spell
until.

Once you've used these tricks to remember your spellings a few times, you'll find they become automatic. So read them through a few times, then have another go at the test ...

... is your spelling cleverer now? Hurray!

If you want to get even cleverer at spelling, or if these examples don't work for you, why not make up some mnemonics yourself?

Here's a reminder of the techniques you could use, along with any others that work for you:
   • spell out the word to a familiar rhythm
   • spell the word out to the tune of a memorable song
   • break down the word into smaller words
   • make up a silly sentence where each letter is the first letter of every word in the sentence
   • use pictures to help you remember any particular letters you get wrong.

Don't 'dis' the dictionary

You don't have to remember how to spell every single word in the English language — that's what dictionaries are for. And dictionaries aren't just there to check your spellings, they'll tell you the meaning of a word too.

So, whenever you come across a word you haven't seen before, or if you don't know its meaning, jot it down in a notebook, and look it up next time you're near a dictionary.

Dictionaries are brilliant for helping you with your vocabulary. Just flicking through them you'll come across all kinds of interesting gems. But if you want to have a bit more fun with a dictionary, try playing this game:

You will need
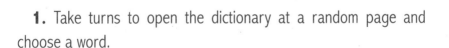
- A dictionary
- A friend
- A timer.

1. Take turns to open the dictionary at a random page and choose a word.

2. Read out the word — then read out a definition. You can either read the definition that goes with the word, or quickly look for another word definition on the same page and read that one out instead. You can lie as much as you like, pretending to read a different definition when you are actually reading the right one, and so on.

3. Your friend then has to work out if the definition is right or not and answer 'True' or 'False' — a correct answer wins them one point, an incorrect answer wins a point for you.

4. Now hand the dictionary over to your friend and start again, keeping note of your scores.

5. After ten minutes, the person with the most points wins.

How to read cleverly

Did you know that reading is one of the very best ways to boost your brainpower? Children who are good at literacy (reading, writing, speaking and listening) are much more likely to grow up to:

- Be happier
- Have good health
- Earn more money
- Get a better job!

Research has shown that reading for fun can increase your chances of getting to university when you're older, because it can help you to learn how to develop opinions, understand emotions as well as arguments, say what you think clearly, and improve your writing skills. Also, if you read and do one other cultural activity, like playing a musical instrument, or going to art galleries and museums, your chances are even higher.

But what can you do if you find reading a bit of a chore? Well, there's got to be at least one book out there on every subject under the sun and you can choose which type of book you want to read. Why not try:

- Non-fiction – teaches you facts and improves your knowledge
- Self-help books – help you to understand yourself better
- Reference books, like dictionaries, or atlases – full of helpful and specific information
- 'How-to' books – help you learn new skills
- Fiction – full of exciting stories to get your imagination going.

Brainbox – comics and graphic novels
Don't let anyone tell you that books with pictures are just for little kids. Did you know that bestselling author Philip Pullman was inspired by comics? This is what he has said about them: "When … my stepfather brought me a Superman comic, it changed my life… I devoured it and demanded more… It was the first stirring of the storytelling impulse."

How to read fiction cleverly

1. You could start by choosing something from the fiction list on p. 57 and 58, or think about subjects you enjoy and in your local library or bookshop for some recommendations.

2. Don't judge a book by its cover. Read the description on the back. Try reading a few pages at random – do you like the style of writing? Do you want to find out more?

3. Get into the habit of always having something to read, and carry your book around with you – it's a great way to look clever!

4. Sometimes it takes a little while to get into a book, but if you find your mind keeps wandering don't force yourself to finish. Maybe you're too tired, or you're not ready for this book yet. Give it a rest, or try something else.

5. When you finish a book, don't just put it down and forget about it. Tell a friend about it, or talk to someone who has also read it. Maybe even ask yourself a few questions:

- Why did I like/hate/feel irritated by this book?
- Why was that character so stupid/evil/fascinating?
- Why did I keep reading/lose interest/have to force myself to finish it?
- Was the ending disappointing/amazing?
- Could I have made the story better?

6. Run though the plot again in your head and test yourself on the names of the characters. If you can remember details of the books you've read months, even years later, people will think you are super clever.

Catching the book bug

Whichever author gets you excited, from Roald Dahl, to Jacqueline Wilson, Jeff Kinney to J. K. Rowling, what matters most is that you enjoy what you read. Once you've caught the book bug, keep experimenting. Try new authors and see what you think. Ask your friends for recommendations, or have a go at the books on this list, they've all been tried and tested by thousands of readers before you:

Ten fiction classics to get your teeth into

1. *Harry and the Wrinklies* – Alan Temperley. When Harry gets sent to live with his great-aunts, he hardly imagines that they're part of a gang ... of cat burglars!

2. *War Horse* – Michael Morpurgo. A First World War story told brilliantly ... from the point of view of a very brave horse!

3. *Winnie-the-Pooh* – A. A. Milne. Don't think *Winnie-the-Pooh* is just for little children. The book is great fun for older children and adults love it too.

4. *A Christmas Carol* – Charles Dickens. It's set at Christmas time, it's got ghosts, and it's written by one of the best British authors of all time. What's not to like?

5. *Goodnight Mister Tom* – Michelle Magorian. It's the Second World War and a young boy from London is sent to live with an angry old man… Will sparks fly?

6. *The Hobbit* – J. R. R. Tolkein. Small, furry-footed and plump, Bilbo Baggins is a hobbit. He doesn't know it yet, but he's about to set off on a life-changing adventure.

7. *Tom's Midnight Garden* – Philippa Pearce. This is a magical story about a boy who discovers a garden that only appears when the clock strikes thirteen.

8. *Harry Potter and the Philosopher's Stone* – J. K. Rowling. The story of a boy who spent the first ten years of his life living under the stairs, until he discovers he's a wizard and his life changes forever.

9. *The Adventures of Huckleberry Finn* – Mark Twain. It was written over 100 years ago, and is about a boy who runs away from home and sails down the Mississippi river with an escaped slave.

10. *The Hundred and One Dalmatians* – Dodie Smith. When the puppies of Missis and Pongo disappear, the two dalmations know that the terrifying Cruella de Vil must be behind it and set off on a daring rescue mission.

Brainbox – audiobooks

Books as good as these are often available as an audiobook. If you're not a big reader then it's great fun listening to a spellbinding story. Listen in the car, before you go to bed, or walking to school. The audio version is sometimes shorter than the original book, so if you find you really like the story then it's definitely worth reading the book too to pick up on any bits you missed.

A clever way to get 'well-read'

If you want to prove to people just how clever you are, it helps if you can say you're 'well read'. This means that you've read a lot of books, but it can also mean that you've seen some Shakespeare plays, know some of the stories from ancient Greece and Rome, or from the Bible and you're familiar with the tales of, say, King Arthur or Robin Hood. Writers often mention bits from other books in their stories, and if you know a few of them already, you might find you pick up on some hidden messages.

Lots of books have been rewritten so they are easier to read or more relevant to readers' today. You can now read Shakespeare plays as comics, or Greek myths as horror stories – even picture books for young children can give you an easy way in to some classic tales. Trying asking in your local library or bookshop and see what you can find.

How to read speedily

It's thought that the average adult reads at a speed of around 150 to 250 words per minute, and that at that speed they can take in around 70% of the information they're reading. If you'd like to read more speedily, there are a few techniques that can help you double your reading rate.

Try the tips below and see if they make a difference. But remember, it's far more important to enjoy and understand what you read than to finish before everyone else.

1. Hand-eye co-ordination can improve your reading ability, so juggling (see p. 120-121), catching or even dancing could help.

2. When you get quite confident with reading, try saying the words in your head instead of mouthing them and you'll soon speed up.

3. Do you use your finger to keep your place while you're reading? That's a great way to read faster. Keeping a ruler under the line as you read is even better. If you can, keep moving it slowly and smoothly down the page without stopping.

Going slow...

While speed is helpful in exams and tests, scientists have found that creativity, and the ability to come up with unusual and different ideas, may be improved if the connections in certain parts of the brain work more slowly.

Similarly, brilliant ideas don't have to be complicated. Often it's the simplest that are the cleverest.

Brain Box – the Green Belt Movement

Wangari Maathai won the Nobel Peace Prize in 2004 … for planting trees.

Wangari was the first woman from East Africa ever to become an academic doctor. Wangari's studies took her around the world, but when she returned to Kenya she was horrified that so many trees had been chopped down to make way for tea or coffee plantations.

The loss of the trees affected whole communities — food was hard to find, and in any case there was no firewood to cook with. The quality of the soil was poor for growing crops and animals were dying out too.

In 1997, Wangari set up the Green Belt Movement and she encouraged women to plant trees with her, explaining as they worked why the trees were so important. The message spread like wildfire, and by the time she died, in 2011, it's estimated 40 million trees had been planted because of her simple, but brilliant campaign.

How to write a great story

If you find writing difficult, then reading can definitely help, but there are other things you can do to make it easier that are lots of fun too.

Which topic to pick?

It's generally best to write about what you know. Do you have a hobby, sport or subject that you love? You could even combine a favourite hobby, with a favourite animal, food or type of story (such as mystery, adventure, science fiction and so on) then try to come up with a title. Maybe you like:

- Elephants + ballet + space
- Robots + skateboards + doughnuts
- Zombies + Tudors + school.

Sometimes having a title can really get you started. You can use your subjects to help you. For example, Zombies + Tudors + school could give you a title like:

Zombie Queen at Back-in-time High

Now start finding out a bit about the Tudors and zombies (you probably know quite a bit about school already). Fill your head with facts and ideas, and get to know as much as you can about your subjects — it all helps with the plot.

Carry a notebook around with you at all times, so you can jot down thoughts and ideas wherever you are and whenever they come to you.

Create a great character

You could write your story from the point of view of your main character – this is called writing in the 'first person'. They might be based on:

- Yourself
- Someone you know well – a teacher, family member or friend
- A character from another story, film or TV show
- All of the above.

Ask yourself some questions about your main character and jot down their key characteristics along the lines of the example below:

Name: Ben Pringle – nickname Bing

Appearance: Quite short for age (11), has dark hair with corkscrew curls, wears glasses. School uniform usually creased; school bag really battered.

Personality: Seems quite ordinary, gets on with people okay. Has a couple of good friends. Could be quite clever if he tried harder.

Enemies: Teacher, Mr Blister — he has got it in for Ben.

Problems: Terrible memory and accident prone.

Unusual quality: Ability to travel back in time (though maybe that's more to do with the school itself).

Working out the plot

A great way to get your plot working is by giving your character a problem, then using it to structure your story.

Beginning: Think of a bold way to start, introducing your character and the 'problem'.

Middle: Show unusual ways your character tries to solve the problem and what happens as a result.

End: Overcome the problem in a surprising way, so you get a really great ending.

Can't work out the whole plot straightaway? No problem, just leave some blanks and come back to them later.

Plot-pinching

If you're really stuck with your storyline you can always pinch bits from someone else's plot. Writers do it all the time and it's okay, particularly if you tell everyone you're doing it:

On the other hand, copying someone else's exact words into your story or homework is an absolute no-no.

Despite there being loads of stories in the world, it has been suggested that actually there are only seven plots, which means there's been an awful lot of plot-pinching going on. To help you get started, here they are:

1. Overcoming the monster – *Jack and the Beanstalk* and *Little Red Riding Hood* are classics.

2. Rags to riches – *Cinderella* is a perfect example.

3. Quest – Stories like *Indiana Jones* and *Harry Potter* are classic quest tales.

4. Voyage and return – If you've read or seen C. S. Lewis's *Chronicles of Narnia: The Lion the Witch and the Wardrobe* you'll recognize this type.

5. Comedy – It doesn't have to be laugh-out-loud funny, but a happy ending is definitely required, like in the film *Shrek*.

6. Tragedy – Someone always dies in the end – Shakespeare's *Hamlet* is probably the most famous tragedy of all time. Disney's *The Lion King* is based on the same story, but has a happy ending instead.

7. Rebirth — Like in a tragedy, the main character behaves badly, but here they realize they're being a pain and change their ways just in time for the story to end … happily! Dickens's *A Christmas Carol* (see p. 57) is a classic rebirth story.

Once your story ideas start taking shape, try planning them out as a Mind Map (see p. 36), like this one:

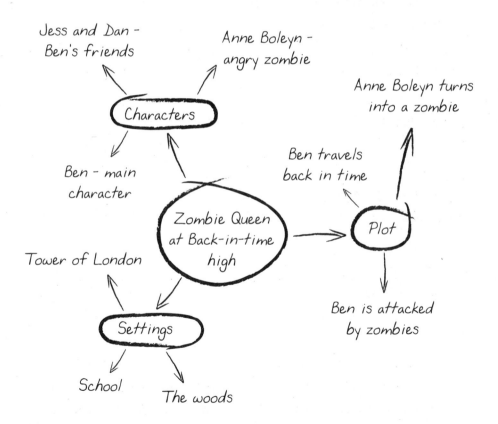

Jess and Dan – Ben's friends

Anne Boleyn – angry zombie

Anne Boleyn turns into a zombie

Characters

Ben travels back in time

Ben – main character

Zombie Queen at Back-in-time high

Plot

Tower of London

Settings

Ben is attacked by zombies

School

The woods

Get writing

So that's the plot sorted, now all you have to do is write out the story! Er, which may not be as easy as it sounds.

You will need

- Your story Mind Map and any other notes
- Lined paper
- Scrap paper
- A pencil
- A rubber.

How to do it

Use lined paper and a pencil for the actual story, and only write on every other line. Having space around your writing means you can come back and change things more easily if you want to.

Try and complete each sentence in your head before you write it down, or try it out on the scrap paper. You might even come up with a few different versions, then you can pick the best one.

Start by setting the scene and getting some important information in there:

Ben was walking to school, he met his friends and they asked if he had done his homework.

Well, as an opening sentence that sets the scene and tells you about the main characters, but it hardly makes you desperate to know more. You could have a go at livening up this sentence by:
- Describing how Ben was walking
- Adding some detail about what sort of day it was
- Saying who his friends are
- Including what Ben's friend said in speech marks
- Adding descriptions of how Ben and his friends look.

There are also other ways to liven up your story and the language you use – just be careful not to overuse these techniques though.

1. Sound effects, or 'onomatopoeia' if you want to sound clever, are a great way to make your story sound more exciting:

Swosh! the axe swooshed through the air. Schlerp! the head slid from the block and thunked to the ground.

You can even have fun making up your own sound effects and noises.

2. Include good descriptive words (adjectives and adverbs):

'Zombie Anne's knobbly, blood-streaked hand reached out shakily and rattled the classroom door handle.'

3. Think about how you put words together – they can sound the same (assonance) or start with the same letter (alliteration):

'Mr Blister cowered in the corner, shaking and quaking with fear.'

Take time writing your story. Keep coming back to it and once you've got it all down on paper, read it through to improve it and check that it makes sense. A good tip is to leave it for a couple of days, then come back and read it again. This time, read it aloud to yourself – that's a great way to pick up on any problems.

As you read, ask yourself:

- What did I mean by that? If I can't understand it no one else will be able to.
- That line sounds a bit weird, have I missed something out?
- How can I make that sentence more exciting?
- Does that word exist in the English language? Help, where's the dictionary?
- It's looking good but how can I make it even better?

If you find you keep using the same words over and over again, try looking for alternatives in the dictionary, or thesaurus. For example, instead of 'It was a bright sunny day,' you could say the day was:

brilliantly/blazingly/dazzingly/splendidly sunny.

When you're happy with your story, ask someone else to read it through for you. Explain that you want them to tell you exactly what they think. Don't go getting upset if they say something you don't like though. Instead, use their comments to improve your story. That's what an editor — someone who helps make your writing as good as possible — is for. Lots of books you've read and loved wouldn't be nearly as good if they hadn't been very well edited.

Using your imagination when you write will help with essays, reports and anything else you have to do for school. And very, very occasionally, children even manage to get their stories published...

Adora Svitak (born 1997)

Reading at two, writing short stories at four and her first book published aged just seven — Adora's achievements didn't stop there. Born in Springfield, Oregon, USA, in 1997, Adora Svitak is an exceptional girl — with an ambition to win a Nobel Prize for Literature or Peace.

It's far more common for children to be gifted at maths or music than literature, but it seems Adora's skill with words is fuelled by her love of reading. She's read well over 1,600 books (some of them several times).

Her first published book, *Flying Fingers*, includes stories and poems, as well as instructions to help parents get their children writing. Teaching is another thing Adora does — she started when she was seven and taught a class at a local school!

Adora's top tip for budding writers is to stop as you get to the middle of your story, write the ending and then go back and finish off the rest of it.

And her mum reckons, with the right support, all children have the potential to be like Adora: reading, writing and doing tests for fun can definitely make you cleverer.

How to be a clever editor

We all make mistakes when writing so you should always, always check your work, whatever you're writing, including homework.

In fact, try to get into the habit of reading through anything you write at least twice. The first read is to see if:

- You've included everything you were supposed to – if it's homework, look back and check you've answered all the questions
- It makes sense
- It's boring to read – if it is, think about how you can make it more interesting.

The second time, read slowly, looking carefully at the words themselves. Keep a ruler under each line and move it down the page as you read to make sure you don't accidentally skip a line. You are looking for:

- Spellings mistakes – keep a dictionary beside you to check anything you're not sure of
- Punctuation problems– have you used capital letters and full stops in the right places?
- Sense – are there any words missing or in the wrong place?
- Consistency – make sure the names of people and places stay the same all the way through.

See if you can you can spot the deliberate mistakes in the paragraph below. There are six of them!

Ben was kicking his rucksack from one leg to the ohter, like it was a football and he was playing keepy-uppy. His dark curls were bouncing up and dwon. Getting to school would take him a while rate at this. Ben spotted Jess and Dan walking Towards him and waved, cheerily. Bert kicked his football towards DAN who tripped over it.

Did you spot them all? Turn the page to find out.

Ben was kicking his rucksack from one leg to the (ohter), like it was a football and he was playing keepy-uppy. His dark curls were bouncing up and (dwon). Getting to school would take him a while (rate at this). Ben spotted Jess and Dan walking (Towards) him and waved, cheerily. (Bert) kicked his football towards (DAN) who tripped over it.

How many did you get?

5-6 – Well done, eagle-eyes – you have the makings of a truly great editor!

3-4 – Not bad. Keep checking your homework like this every time and you'll soon see an improvement.

0-2 – Don't worry, this is why it's good to practise. Go back and have another look. Remember to read slowly and circle anything you're not sure about.

BE CLEVER AT MATHS

A clever way to be really good at maths is to know your times tables from one to ten or, even better, from one to 12. Tables aren't difficult — it's just a question of remembering them. That generally means learning them off by heart by repeating them again and again. But your teachers probably told you that there are short cuts that will make this much easier. They didn't? Well, here you are, you need never be stuck on your tables again...

6 8 10 12 14 16 18 20 22 24 26 28 30 32 34 36 38 4

Times tables tricks
Ones
Okay, you probably already know your one times table:

   1 x 1=1, 2 x 1=2 and so on.

Twos
And you've learnt your two times table because, of course, all you have to do is double the number, or add it to itself, and you've got the answer:

   $2 \times 2 = 2 + 2 = 4$
   $12 \times 2 = 12 + 12 = 24$ and so on.

Fives
Let's skip to your five times table because it is pretty straightforward too. Every number in the five times table must end with either a five or a zero, so practising counting in fives is helpful and not that hard.

   5, 10, 15, 20, 25, 30, 35 ...

Ah, but there's a problem with just counting it out — you know that 45 is part of the five times table because it has a five at the end. But how many times can five be divided into 45? Without knowing the whole calculation, it's difficult to remember.

Fancy finding out a quick way to work it out without using your fingers? Here's what you do:

Double the number: $45 + 45 = 90$
(If you've doubled it properly, it will always end in zero.)
Take off the zero and, hey presto, your answer is 9!

The same trick works with larger numbers, too — 525 ends in a five, so it can be divided by five. But how many times does five go into 525?

Double the number: $525 + 525 = 1050$
Take off the zero, and there's your answer: 105
$105 \times 5 = 525$
$525 \div 5 = 105$

Tens

Next let's move on to your ten times table – any problems? Thought not. With tens, the numbers just move one place across the number columns – from units, to tens, then to hundreds and so on – and a zero shows where it used to be:

H T U (Hundreds, tens, units)
   $9 \times 10 =$
  9 0

H T U
   $7 \, 0 \times 10 =$
  7 0 0

Nines

The nine times table might look difficult, but actually, there are lots of tricks for this one. For instance, did you know that all the numbers in the nine times table add up to nine when you add their digits together? Though you might have to do a couple of steps:

$2 \times 9 = 18 \ldots 1 + 8 = 9$
$4 \times 9 = 36 \ldots 3 + 6 = 9$
$24 \times 9 = 216 \ldots 2 + 1 + 6 = 9$

It works with even larger numbers, too:

43 x 9 = 387 ... 3 + 8 + 7 = 18 ... 1 + 8 = 9
652 x 9 = 5868 ... 5 + 8 + 6 + 8 = 27 ... 2 + 7 = 9

And, if a large number will add up to nine, you can definitely divide it by nine too:

459 (4 + 5 + 9 = 18 ... 1 + 8 = 9) ÷ 9 = 51
702 (7 + 2 = 9) ÷ 9 = 78

For the best trick with the nine times table you're going to need your fingers. All ten of them. Each of your fingers represents a number from one to ten.

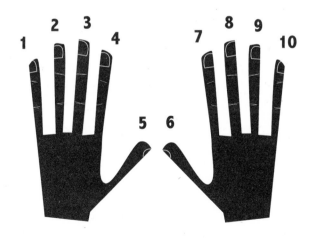

To help you work out the nine times table – 4 x 9, for example – simply fold down the finger number four, like this:

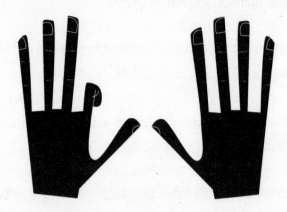

With fingers on the left of the bent finger as tens, and the fingers on the right as units, this means that 4 x 9 = 36 – easy, isn't it? Try it out with the rest of the nine times table – it really works.

Elevens

Your eleven times table up to ten is a doddle, too. You are basically multiplying a number by ten and then by one, so you end up with two of the original number you multiplied by:

$3 \times 11 = (3 \times 10 = 30) + (3 \times 1 = 3) = 33$
$7 \times 11 = (7 \times 10 = 70) + (7 \times 1 = 7) = 77$

It all seems to change when you get to multiplying by double digits, but there's still a clever trick you can use.

To multiply 10 x 11 add the two digits of the number you're multiplying 11 by together: $1 + 0 = 1$. Put the result in the middle of the two-digit number you started with — 110 — and that's your answer!

$10 \times 11 = 110$

The same trick works with all double figures, although some need a little more calulation. For instance:

$59 \times 11 - 5 + 9 = 14$ but you don't put 14 between 5 and 9. Instead, the second digit, 4, goes between 5 and 9, and you add the first digit, 1, to the 5. So the answer is 649.

74 x 11 = (7 + 4 = 11 – so put the 1 in the middle and add 1 to the first digit) = 814

And did you know that if you write out any number, 297, for example, and then write it backwards to make one long number – 297792 – it is very probably divisible by 11!

Twelves

The twelve times table is easier if you multiply by ten first, then multiply by two and add your answers together:

8 x 12 = (10 x 8 = 10) + (2 x 8 = 16) = 96
7 x 12 = (10 x 7 = 70) + (2 x 7 = 14) = 84

Threes and fours

The three and four times tables aren't so hard to remember, though if you're stuck on your fours, you can always do the two times table first, then double it.

12 x 4 = 2 x 12 + 2 x 12 = 24 + 24 = 48

And with threes you can double the number then add it again.

3 x 12 = 12 x 2 = 24 + 12 = 36

Sixes, sevens and eights

It's not hard to learn most times tables, especially because you start by learning the twos, threes and fours. But for some reason, we always leave the trickiest ones till last … the sixes, sevens and eights…

There is a trick for the sixes, but it only works with even numbers:

6 x 2 = 12

When the answer is an even number, the last digit of the number you multiply by is the same as the last digit in your answer, so:

6 x 6 = 36 – you multiplied by six so the last digit is six
6 x 12 = 72 – you multiplied by 12 so the last digit is two

But in fact, by the time you come to learn these nasty tables, you really already know most of them. You've done your ones to fives and your nines and tens, so the trickier calculations of all are those where sixes, sevens and eights are multiplied by each other.

6 x 6 = 36 (remember the trick)
6 x 7 = 42
6 x 8 = 48 (remember the trick)
7 x 7 = 49
7 x 8 = 56 (this goes in sequence — 56 = 7 x 8)
8 x 8 = 64

There they are — all six of them. So the good news is, if you use a few tricks to master the rest of your tables, the only ones you really have to learn are these. Learn them really well. Write them down, stick them on the wall, put them on the bathroom mirror while you're brushing your teeth … if you can rattle out these answers the second you're asked, everyone is going to think you're super clever!

Can you count to one billion?

It doesn't sound all that difficult, does it? We know how numbers work, and we know all the numbers we need to get there. But how big is a billion really?

How quickly can you count to 100? Go on, time yourself. With a bit of practice you can probably do it quite fast. Say in 30 seconds or less. You'd probably have to slow down a little after that, as the numbers take longer to say.

However, let's assume you can count 100 numbers a minute. Without taking a loo break or stopping to eat or sleep, yawn or die of boredom, you would reach one million in around six days, 22 hours and 40 minutes. So you see, one million is a pretty big number, isn't it?

You might think, then, that counting to one billion would take a good few weeks. Your counting will slow down because of the time it takes to say really long numbers (nine hundred and forty-five million, four thousand five hundred and seventy-two takes a lot longer to say than plain old four thousand five hundred and seventy-two). So even if you count at a rate of one number per second (you'd still need to count pretty fast), it's going to take very nearly 32 YEARS, (and that's with no loo breaks, no sleep and no losing count at any time)!

Numbers don't stop at billions though. And luckily, with all those noughts, there is a short way of writing them:

1,000 x 1,000 = 1,000,000 (1 million) or 10^{6*}
1,000 x 1,000,000 = 1,000,000,000 (1 billion) or 10^9
1,000 x 1,000,000,000 = 1,000,000,000,000 (1 trillion) or 10^{12}

You've probably heard of trillions, but did you know about quadrillions (10^{15}) quintillions (10^{18}) or even centillions (10^{303})?

You could go on counting just about forever, but you've probably got better things to do. In any case, when are you likely to use these numbers?

— - **1, 2, 3, 4, 5, 6, 7, 8, 9, 10, 11, 12, 13, 14, 15, 16, 17, 1**

*That little '6' means ten to the power of six, which means you multiply 10 by itself 6 times:
10 x 10 x 10 x 10 x 10 x 10 = 1,000,000

Well probably not as often as you'd count from one to 100, but, for example, it's thought:

- There are 350,000 different species of beetle on earth — so how many beetles must there be altogether?
- Zimbabwe printed its first 100 trillion dollar note in 2009 — it was worth about £20
- The earth is 15 billion years old (if it takes nearly 32 years to count to one billion ... then 15 billion years is a very long time indeed)
- 50-100 trillion cells make up a human body
- Each galaxy in the universe contains on average of 100 billion to one trillion stars
- There may be up to one septillion (10^{24}) stars in the universe.

While you may not use these numbers a lot today, as populations grow (see p. 148), as the value of money increases and as we find out more about the universe, it might be a clever idea to get to know them a little bit better.

Famously clever: Karl Friedrich Gauss (1777-1855)

Karl Friedrich Gauss was one of the greatest mathematicians of all time, and it showed even from an early age. Karl didn't go to school until he was seven and his intelligence didn't get noticed immediately. But one day his teacher asked everyone in the class to add up all the numbers from one to 100, write down their final answer and put it on his desk when they had finished.

Instead of adding one number to the next, as the other boys were doing, Karl spotted a short cut. He quickly worked out that if he laid the numbers out in two rows (but he did this without writing them down!), so that one was over 100, and two was over 99 – each pair of numbers added up to 101.

$$
\begin{array}{ccccccc}
1 & 2 & 3 & 4 & 5 & \ldots \\
+\,100 & +\,99 & +\,98 & +\,97 & +\,96 & \ldots \\
\hline
101 & 101 & 101 & 101 & 101 &
\end{array}
$$

To get the final answer, he just had to multiply 101, by the total number of calculations, which was 50.

Within minutes, Karl wrote down '5050' and laid his answer on the teacher's desk. The rest of the class slaved on, slowly adding one number to the next. Karl finished first by miles, and had the correct answer.

He probably didn't know it at the time, but Karl had discovered an 'algorithm'*. He wasn't the first person ever to find one, but most people don't automatically use them at the age of ten!

It's hardly surprising then that Karl went on to make amazing discoveries in the fields of geometry (the study of angles and lines), and astronomy (the study of stars and planets). He was a perfectionist and very careful about sharing his ideas though. One expert claimed that if all Gauss's findings had been published when he wrote about them, maths would have advanced by 50 years.

Karl Gauss may be gone, but he's certainly not forgotten. His face has appeared on bank notes, stamps and buildings – he's even had a crater on the moon named after him!

* An algorithm is a way of solving a problem using specific, time-saving steps.

Music can definitely make you cleverer!

Now, if you want to be really clever at maths, try playing a musical instrument. According to one report, students studying music scored 15% higher in a maths test than another group who had been playing a maths video game.

In 1993, a team of researchers ran tests, which — they said — proved that listening to Mozart, rather than other types of music, could improve a student's ability to work out a sequence of patterns. Before the ink had dried on the research papers, the story had hit the headlines. The world was delighted. At last — a pain-free way to boost the brain cells! Sales of Mozart CDs soared, his music was

...d to students and school children alike, and in Florida, USA, became law for state day-care centres to broadcast an hour of Mozart each day to its children.

Unfortunately, the newspapers were getting carried away. Other researchers tried the tests and never got the same results. But, a study of 10-11 year olds in the UK found that listening to pop music before starting your homework could improve performance for up to 10-15 minutes. Researchers thought this was because listening to something you enjoy is stimulating and energizing, so you start your studies in a better frame of mind.

There's a much better and longer-lasting way to improve your brain through music though and that's by making the music yourself! Yes, we're talking lessons here: piano, guitar, drums, ukulele, cello, trombone ... even learning to sing properly (not just singing into a hairbrush) can seriously boost your brain.

So the facts are all there, but don't worry if you don't already play an instrument, you can start at any age, you can even start right now...

Keyboard lesson
Start at the very beginning

WARNING: If you have never played any music before, you might need to take your time over this lesson. Read everything through a few times and take it in stages if you like. Don't worry if it doesn't fall into place straightaway.

You will need

- Your fingers
- This book
- A keyboard — piano or electric, it doesn't matter which.

If you don't have one, ask your school, friendly neighbours or local community centre if you can use theirs.

Getting started

A piece of music looks like this:

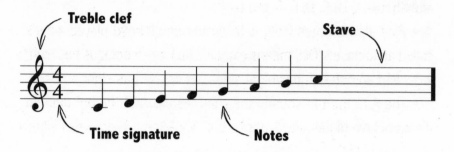

Clef – this shows which part of the piano the notes are to be played on. The two main clefs are:

Treble clef – used by instruments like the flute and recorder that play high-sounding notes. On the piano, the treble clef is used for notes above middle C – the note found in the middle of the piano.

Bass clef – used by instruments like the cello and tuba that play low-sounding notes. On the piano, the bass clef is used for notes below middle C.

Time signature – shows how many beats are in a bar – this time signature is 4/4, which means there are four crotchets in a bar (see p. 100)

Stave – this is the series of lines that notes are written on

Note – the dots on the stave are notes, there are different notes for every white and black key on the piano. Notes above and below the stave have lines through them to show which notes they are.

Here's how the notes work:

- Musical notes are represented by the first seven letters of the alphabet — A, B, C, D, E, F and G.

- Play all the notes from A to A, and you'll have played what's called an 'octave'. 'Oct' means eight, so just as an octopus has eight legs, and an octagon has eight sides, an octave has eight notes.

- The A at the top sounds the same as the A at the bottom, but it's an octave higher, the A above that would be two octaves higher.

Now you know what a piece of music looks like and what each bit is for, you need to learn which notes are which. Luckily, there are a few tricks you can use to make things easier:

In the treble clef, the notes in the spaces, F, A, C and E, spell out the word 'face'.

The notes on the lines, E, G, B, D and F, can be remembered with the phrase — Every Good Boy Deserves Fivers.

F   A   C   E   E   G   B   D   F

The length of a note, or the beat, is shown with these symbols.

♪   **Quaver** – ½ a beat, made up of ½ a crotchet

♩   **Crotchet** – 1 beat

𝅗𝅥   **Minim** – 2 beats, made up of 2 crotchets

𝅗𝅥.   **Dotted-minim** – 3 beats, made up of 3 crotchets

𝅝   **Semibreve** – 4 beats, made up of 4 crotchets

When put on a stave, the notes look like this:

In this example, there are four beats in every bar, but the notes are played for different lengths of time. When quavers are shown together their 'tails' are joined.

You might want to look through those diagrams a few times, very carefully. It's tricky and takes people a long time to learn to play the piano, so don't worry if it's all a bit puzzling to start with, just keep practising. Got it? Good!

So, drumroll please, you need to prepare to put some notes together with the keyboard, and the keyboard together with your fingers. Ready?

Hold up your right hand:

See how each finger in the picture is numbered from 1 to 5?

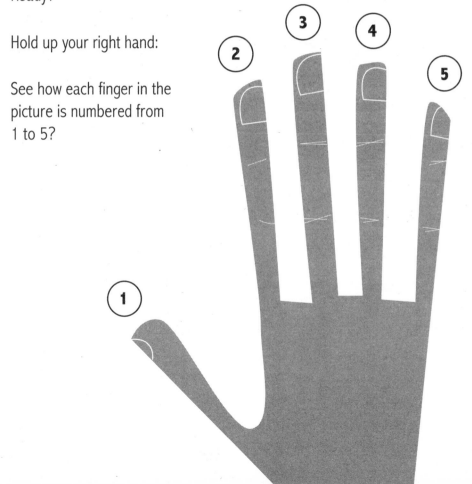

Now look at the keyboard. Notice the pattern of the notes. An octave looks like this:

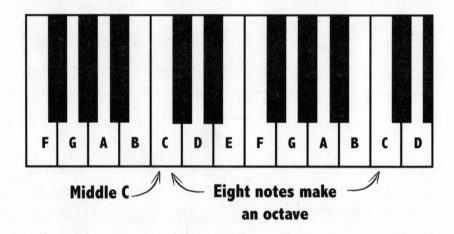

Middle C —⤻   ⤻— **Eight notes make —⤻**
                                an octave

The 'C' that's closest to the middle of a full piano keyboard is called 'middle C'. That's where you need to start.

The black keys are called sharps and flats, but don't worry about those just now.

Put your right thumb (number one) on middle 'C' and the rest of your fingers on the notes that come after it – D, E, F and G. So each numbered finger sits on the note shown in the diagram.

Let's start playing

Now look at this little tune:

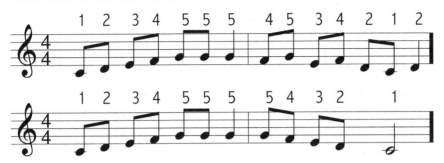

The whole tune uses just five notes — one for each finger — so you don't need to worry about moving your hand from this position. As the notes move up the stave, your fingers move up the keyboard. If you're not sure about this, just make sure your hand is in the correct position, and try following the numbers above the notes — or the 'fingering' as it's called.

Are you getting the idea?

Concentrate on getting the notes right first. Keep playing and playing them, until your fingers feel comfortable on the keys and you're getting to know the tune. You don't need to worry about the timing just yet...

Now you've got the hang of the notes, look back at them again. Can you work out how long each one should last?

Remember there are four beats to each bar — you can tell this because of the 4/4 shown at the start of the music. Try tapping your foot on the floor with a slow, regular beat (or ask someone else to do it for you). One — two — three — four. Everything in the bar should last for four beats only. The first bar has six quavers and one crotchet (look back to the note lengths on p. 100, if you need reminding). Each quaver will last the same length of time. For each tap of your foot you will need to play two notes.

In the second bar again, you will need to play two notes for each of the first three beats because there are six quavers, and then one note for the fourth beat because the note is a crotchet. Can you work out the rest of the tune? It's not as hard as it sounds, honest!

Keep on playing the tune until the rhythm feels just about right, and you're finding it easier each time you play it.

Phew! Quite hard work, isn't it? You can see how music exercises your brain! Take a break now if you like, but remember to come back and practise the tune again and again.

On the other hand...

If you're feeling really keen, you could have a go at jazzing up the tune yourself:

- If you've got a keyboard with different settings, try out some different styles.
- Try changing the rhythm, by making some of the notes a little longer or shorter.
- You could experiment with the tune by mixing the notes up a bit. Keep your hand in the same position, but just try changing the notes here and there and see how it sounds.
- Try making up your own tune, keeping those five fingers on the same keys, or adding in notes A and B if you like.

Wow! If managed to do any one of those, you've done really brilliantly and you've certainly worked your brain. If you've impressed mum and dad, serenaded the hamster and enjoyed playing around with a keyboard, maybe it's time to ask about proper lessons? And if your parents need some persuading, here's a story that might help you.

What music lessons could do for you

On a visit to Germany in the 1940s, the Japanese violinist Dr Shinichi Suzuki was impressed by the fact that, although as an adult he found German a difficult language, German children could speak it quickly and easily from a very young age. It made him wonder whether children could learn the language of music just as easily, and so he started to develop 'Talent Education'.

He wanted to teach children that to be talented at music you didn't have to show any special abilities to begin with. He believed that all children are born with different abilities, but their experiences affect the way they develop. His method included:

• Listening to music before starting to play (so pupils get to know their pieces really well)

• Playing music before learning to read

• Getting parents involved (to make sure their children practise).

Suzuki got some children playing at just two and three years old! He said that music teaches "sensitivity, discipline and endurance" that would help children to grow up to be "fine human beings, happy people, people of superior ability". Recent tests have also shown that children who learn music can develop better memories and improve their literacy and maths, There are now over 8,000 Suzuki teachers around the world.

Famously clever: Wolfgang Amadeus Mozart (1756-1791) and Maria Anna Mozart (1751-1829)

Leopold Mozart was a successful court musician, music teacher and composer, so when his first child was just eight years old, it made sense to teach her the harpsichord. Maria Anna Mozart, nicknamed Nannerl, made fantastic progress and her dad even boasted she was "...one of the most skilful players in Europe."

Little brother, Wolfgang Amadeus, was only three when Maria Anna started learning, and just big enough to pull himself up onto the harpsichord stool.

Wolfgang was so keen, he started music lessons when he was just four and progressed even faster than his brilliant sister. By the time he was five, he'd already performed in public. Both children wrote music, and Maria Anna helped Wolfgang to complete his first symphony at the age of eight!

Keen to show off his talented children, Leopold took Maria Anna, aged 11, and Wolfgang, aged six, on a bumpy, horse and carriage tour of Europe. Over three and a half years, they performed to thousands of people – kings and queens included.

While Wolfgang got more and more of his father's attention, Maria Anna eventually stopped performing altogether. Why? Well, she was a girl, and once she was 18, like all other girls her age at the time, she was expected to get married.

Things didn't go too well for Wolfgang, though. As he grew up, he stopped being a cute kid and had to work really hard to make a living. It didn't help that he was hopeless with money as well.

During his lifetime, Wolfgang composed over 600 pieces of music, including an incredible 41 symphonies, around 30 concertos and over 20 operas, not to mention quartets, choral works and chamber music, much of which is still played today. So you might think he must have lived a very long life. Actually, he died quite suddenly, aged just 35, and because he still owed money, poor Wolfgang was buried in a pauper's grave.

What about the clever girls?

Many people think that if Maria Anna Mozart had been given the same attention as her brother, she might have achieved just as much.

Looking back through history, women of the past weren't usually given much choice. They were expected to stay at home, get married, have a family, cook the tea, do the washing... They usually weren't allowed to study, but there were some exceptions:

Albert Einstein met his first wife, Mileva Maric, when he was at technical college. She was the only woman on his course. Her parents had only allowed her to study because she had a limp and they didn't think anyone would want to marry her! It's thought Mileva helped Albert to develop his ideas, but if she did, she never got much credit for it.

There were 1,825 men and 23 women studying at the Sorbonne (a university in Paris), when Marie Curie attended. Marie went on to win a Nobel prize for Physics with her husband, for discovering radioactivity, and on her own for Chemistry. Between 1901 and 2011, 549 Nobel prizes have been awarded, but of those only 44 were given to women.

Over the last 20 years in the UK, girls have regularly scored higher than boys in exams. But in the past, men claimed that women just weren't as clever as men. Sometimes women had to behave and even dress more like men, in order to be noticed for their intelligence. Women writers have often published their books under a man's name instead of their own. George Eliot, author of seven books including *Middlemarch* was in fact called Mary Ann Evans.

BE CLEVER ABOUT ART

Have you ever listened to adults talking about art or seen a person on TV sounding clever and wondered whether you're looking at the same painting? Knowing, or sounding like you know, about art, is a sure way to make yourself seem clever, but where do you begin?

When you first look at a painting, it's good to work out your own feelings about it. Do you like it? Is it interesting, ugly, shocking, well-painted? Does it look real? What effect does it have on you?

Actually, understanding art is often much easier if you know something about the artist and the things that have influenced them. Take Frida Kahlo, for example...

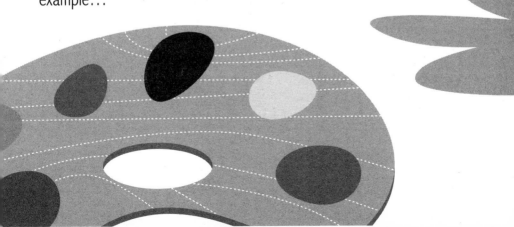

Famously clever: Frida Kahlo (1907-1954)

She is now probably Mexico's best-known artist, but Frida had to overcome many setbacks in her short life to achieve success. When she was just six years old she got a disease called polio and was left with a permanent limp. To recover, she was encouraged to swim, wrestle, climb trees and play football. This didn't stop Frida from working hard at school though. She was one of just a few girls at Mexico City's National Preparatory School, and hoped to become a doctor one day ... but she never made it.

In 1925, Frida was in a dreadful traffic accident that left her with terrible injuries — she had to wear painful corsets and plaster casts for the rest of her life. She spent months recovering from her accident and during this time she started to paint — using a mirror, and herself as her main subject, as she was often alone. Throughout her life she painted hundreds of pictures, mostly self- portraits and still lifes, in a deliberately childlike and colourful style. Today her paintings sell for more money than any other female artist in the world.

So what's her style? A French writer and poet called André Breton told Frida that her work was 'Surrealist'. This was news to Frida, who hadn't thought she fitted any particular mould.

Style files

But works of art are often described according to their style, so it helps to know what some of them are:

Style: Renaissance

How to recognize: Look for amazing use of light and shade, 3D objects, scenes and people. 'Perspective' was the buzz word of the Renaissance artists. They painted and sculpted people and objects, so that they seemed in exact proportion to the world around them.

What's it all about? Italian artists Michelangelo and Leonardo da Vinci are the most famous Renaissance artists. They thought that Medieval art was so 'yesterday' and wanted to create a fabulous new style that had depth and detail. They looked back to the art of Ancient Greece and Rome, but used ground-breaking new 15th century techniques and materials. The new-fangled oil paints they used made their paintings look more realistic.

What to say about it: "Gasp! It's so real, I could almost pick that apple out of the picture and eat it."

Style: Impressionism

How to recognize: Don't get too close! You won't be able to see what you're looking at. It's best to stand back to observe these pictures properly.

Instead of going for the 'everything as real as possible' approach, this style gives an 'impression' of the scene. It might include ordinary looking people in beautiful outdoor scenes. The colours are vivid and bright and painted on the canvas with quick, short brush strokes.

What's it all about? Claude Monet painted the first Impressionist painting in France in the 1870s. Some critics thought Monet's paintings didn't look finished, but Monet wasn't bothered. He was far more interested in the effects he could achieve with light and colour.

What to say about it: "Of course, I haven't a clue what it is, but the 'juxtaposition'* of the colours is enchanting. And look! The paint is so thick you can actually see the brush strokes."

* 'Juxtaposition' is a word art critics love to use. It refers to the way an artist puts opposite things together.

Style: Cubism

How to recognize: You might not see what the image is straightaway. The picture is made up of shapes such as tubes, cylinders and cones. The artist might look at his subject from different angles and show more than one angle at the same time. So in a portrait, instead of the person looking forward or to the side, a cubist picture might show both poses.

What's it all about? Pablo Picasso and Georges Braque developed Cubism as a different approach to art. Instead of following the styles of European painters, they looked for new influences like, say, an African tribal mask.

What to say about it: "I love the way the artist has fragmented and reconstructed the object. I'd never considered a teapot in quite that way before."

Style: Surrealism

How to recognize: It probably includes objects or animals that are familiar, but they're either out of place, doing something strange, or painted to look a bit weird. The pictures might include optical illusions — look at it once and you think you can see a group of people, but look again and you realize the people are piles of rocks.

What's it all about? Surrealists, like René Magritte and Salvador Dali, were fascinated with the stuff going on inside their heads, not just what they saw in the world around them. Surrealism developed around the time that a psychoanalyst named Sigmund Freud was coming up with his theories about the subconscious – and how dreams affected people's waking lives.

What to say about it: "Hmm, ... those clocks look so real, and yet they are melting just like cheese. Maybe the artist is suggesting that time plays tricks on us all?"

Apart from Renaissance art, the styles described here all come under the title 'Modern Art'. Modern Art includes paintings that were completed 130 years ago to the present day. Art can be confusing. Of course, there are lots more artistic styles too. You might want to find out about Romanticism, Modernism, Classicism, Neoclassicism and many others.

But why do people get so excited about a load of marks on a canvas? Well, looking at art is a way of seeing things through someone else's eyes. Artists are always searching for new ways to view the world. They can help you to think differently or understand different ideas. One report on children studying art, even found that talking about art can improve writing ability.

Now you know some basic facts, why not hop on down to your local art gallery and see what you can see? Don't worry about whether or not you understand a picture. Picasso once said: "What I want is that my picture should evoke nothing but emotion." And Salvador Dali claimed he didn't understand his own paintings: "…just because I don't know the meaning of my art, does not mean it has no meaning…"

If you really want to appreciate art, look for paintings you really like, then try to find out a bit about them and the artists who made them, and think about what they mean to you.

OTHER WAYS TO BE CLEVER

Believe it or not, juggling is astonishingly brilliant brain-training. In an experiment in 2009, scientists asked 24 grown-up volunteers to spend half an hour a day teaching themselves to juggle, and 24 other grown-ups to do the same as they always do — and not juggle.

The scientists scanned all 48 brains before and after the juggling practice. Those who had learned to juggle had improved the signals, or white matter, in the 'parietal lobe' — the area of the brain that connects the things we see with the way we move.

Best of all, the research showed that:
* You didn't have to be good at juggling, it was the learning process that mattered
* The change in the brain was permanent, even if you didn't carry on juggling regularly
* Learning other new skills, like a language, or how to ride a unicycle will help too.

Anyway, we mustn't waste time discussing it, let's get juggling now!

How to juggle

First choose your balls. You'll need three tennis balls, oranges or potatoes ... but proper juggling balls, or even bean bags (they don't roll so far) are ideal.

Start with just the one ball, and stand like this:

If you're right-handed, throw from your right hand first, if you're left-handed throw from your left.

Throw the ball up, so that it rises just above your nose, and then starts to fall, so it's easy to catch with the other hand. Practise this again and again ... and again and again.

Next, stand as you did before, but with a ball in each hand. Throw the first ball up and across, then as it starts to fall, throw the second ball in the opposite direction.

Lift your arm up to throw and lower it to catch.

TOP TIP: To stop balls flying all over the place, you might find it's easier to stand in front of a bare wall — so the balls won't roll so far when you drop them.

When, you're absolutely sure you can throw two balls, you can start again with TWO balls in one hand, and one ball in the other.

Throw the first ball just as you did before, and release the second ball when the first one starts to fall. Catch the first ball, then as the second ball starts to fall, release the third ball.

Did the balls go anywhere near your hands? Don't worry if they didn't, juggling takes lots of practice.

Now, try to throw all three balls once, twice, three times. Keep on trying. Eventually you'll find you can juggle for longer and longer.

If you keep on dropping the balls all over the place, remember, the volunteers in the experiment did this for half an hour a day for six weeks – and some became much better jugglers than others. Don't give up, because the best thing is, like riding a bike or swimming, once you've learned to juggle, you'll never forget how to do it.

Brain box – learn a language

Being bilingual – speaking two languages fluently – is brilliant, because it's as if your brain is working out all the time and you don't even notice! Regularly choosing which language you need to use means that, in certain situations, you become quicker than others who only speak one language. You can focus better, and you pick up other languages more easily.

Even if you're not bilingual, learning a language is great for your brain. Of course, it's fantastic for trips abroad, but even if you stay at home, it will stretch your brain in new directions. So grab the chance to learn a language at school, and help yourself to improve, by checking out foreign language CDs and TV programmes, or trying a beginner's course online.

Not thinking can make you cleverer!

If your brain is feeling a bit tired from all that bilingual thinking, why not try not thinking at all? Tests have shown that meditating can really improve your memory, concentration and reaction times. Tibetan monks have been meditating for thousands of years, but Western scientists are only just starting to catch on.

Meditation is about trying to quieten the thoughts that go on in your brain most of the time you're awake.

When someone meditates it looks like they're not doing anything at all, but in fact meditation is amazing exercise for the brain. And just as your muscles build up by regularly lifting heavy weights, parts of the prefrontal cortex* in your brain can thicken and strengthen through regular meditation 'workouts' too.

But, you don't have to be as experienced as a Tibetan monk to feel the benefits of meditation. Research has shown that even people who haven't ever meditated before can improve their brain in certain ways once they start.

So how do you do it? There are lots of different ways to meditate and, to learn properly, it's probably best to go to a class with an experienced teacher. You can have a go at home, though. And if you've got a friend you can trust not to giggle too much, you could even try meditating together.

Meditate in the morning, if you can, when your brain is alert and awake. And if you find you like it, keep practising at the same time each day. Start with five minutes, building up to ten minutes a day once you've got the hang of it.

If you're worried about timing yourself, set a gentle alarm to remind you to stop after five or ten minutes.

* The part of the brain that helps you to think, plan, solve problems and learn new tasks.

Are you sitting comfortably?

First, you need to find somewhere quiet, where you won't be disturbed, that isn't too hot or too cold. It's best to wear loose clothes (pyjamas are perfect). Sit on the floor with your legs crossed and pop a cushion under your bottom to keep your back straight. Relax your jaw, so your teeth aren't touching and close your eyes.

Now, think about your breathing. For meditation you need to keep your breathing regular ... slow and deep.

Close your eyes and focus on your breathing. Now, deeply and slowly, breathe in ... breathe out... Count to one, making each breath an even length.

Breathe in ... breathe out... Count to two as you breathe in and breathe out.

Breathe in ... breathe out... Count to three on each breath. Keep going like this until you reach ten, making your breath longer each time, then start again from one. Don't panic and stop breathing if you can't make it to ten, find a number you feel comfortable with and practise making your breath longer each time you meditate.

If you feel your mind drifting, push the thoughts away and pull your attention back to your breathing and start counting again from one.

And relax...

That's it! How do you feel? Relaxed, calm, head clear, ready to get on with the day? Well, it might not happen straightaway, but that's the feeling you're aiming for. Keep practising and you'll soon start to get it. Though it'll take an awful lot of practice to be as good as...

• •

Famously clever: the Dalai Lama (born 1935)

In 1935, a boy called Lhamo Dhondup was born in a small village in Tibet. His mum and dad were farmers and had several children. But when he was two years old, a search party of Buddhist monks arrived and believed that Lhamo Dhondup was the reincarnation of the 13th Dalai Lama. This meant the little boy was the 14th Dalai Lama and his life was about to change forever.

For the Dalai Lama, education began at six, and continued until he was 25. But at 16, on top of his studies, he also became Head of State for Tibet. In 1959, China invaded and took over Tibet, and the Dalai Lama was forced to flee to India where he has lived ever since.

Even though he lives in India, he's never forgotten his duty to the Tibetan people and today he travels the world, spreading a message of peace. In 1989, the Dalai Lama was awarded the Nobel Peace Prize for his "... resistance to the use of violence in his people's struggle to regain their liberty".

The name Dalai Lama, means 'Ocean of Wisdom', and wisdom is a combination of knowledge and experience that comes over time. That's what Lhamo Dhondup gained from studying and meditating from such an early age. He also learned to use the teachings of the past, while keeping up with modern ideas — he even has a Twitter account! Most importantly, he learned to think differently.

Sleep yourself clever

Once upon a time, people used to go to bed when it got dark, and get up when it was light. Candles and light bulbs changed all that, and now TV and computers encourage us to sleep less and less.

But not getting enough shut-eye can affect your brain, causing poor concentration and slowing progress at school, which certainly isn't clever.

Brainbox – sleep
Are you getting enough? Check here to find out. Answer yes or no to each of the following questions:

- Do you have trouble waking up in the mornings?

  Yes/No

- Do you sometimes sleep through the alarm clock?

  Yes/No

- Are you always yawning at breakfast?

  Yes/No

- Do you often have itchy eyes?

  Yes/No

- Do you find yourself nodding off in class?

  Yes/No

If you answered 'yes' to three or more of these questions, then you definitely need more sleep!

The right amount of sleep is absolutely essential to your health and well-being. Get your sleep patterns just right, and you are likely to:

- Be more alert
- Solve problems better
- Think more creatively
- Remember things better.

According to experts, most adults should be getting a full eight hours, while you should be aiming for a good ten hours sleep. So how can you guarantee a good night's sleep?

Dos and don'ts for a good night's sleep:

DO pack plenty of action into your day – every hour you spend sitting down adds three minutes to the time it takes you to get to sleep!

DO start winding down about an hour before bedtime. Try having a warm bath or reading a story (see p. 57-58).

DO turn out the lights — it's easier to get to sleep in the dark.

DO go to bed at the same time every night — and get up at the same time each morning. Your body likes a regular routine.

DO keep a notebook and pen by the side of your bed. Jot down any niggling thoughts ... and then put them right out of your mind.

DON'T charge about just before going to sleep, your body will wake up just when you want it to relax.

DON'T keep a computer or TV in your bedroom, or if you do, make sure it goes off at least an hour before you go to sleep.

DON'T eat, or drink fizzy drinks, just before you go to bed.

DON'T even drink hot chocolate — like the fizzy drinks, it's full of sugar and can wake you up.

DON'T bother counting sheep. Scientists say it's too boring to help you sleep. Imagining a relaxing scene is much more effective.

Famously clever: Thomas Edison (1847-1931)

American-born Thomas Edison didn't waste much time with school, spending around three months there in total. His teacher didn't like him very much because he constantly asked questions, so his mum took him out of school and taught him herself.

At the age of 12, Edison already had a job selling newspapers at the local railway station – he read them from cover to cover in his spare time. With his hard-earned cash he bought equipment so he could print a newspaper and sell it to passengers along the line.

Edison moved from working on the railway, and trained as a telegraph operator. At the time, the telegraph was the only way to send messages at speed over long distances, and Edison soon invented successful ways to improve the system.

At 21, Edison set up a laboratory and factory to develop his many ideas. He wanted to work on inventions that would benefit ordinary people. Today he's particularly remembered for developing the light bulb, the phonograph (an early machine for recording sound) and a film camera and projector. But, altogether during his lifetime it's thought Edison worked on around 1,300 inventions!

Can eating help you get a better brain?

Food probably won't make you cleverer, but scientists reckon it can have a positive effect on your brain. By following their findings, you could make …

… a Clever Sandwich

You will need

- Wholegrain bread (the wholegrain bit helps improve blood-flow to your brain)
- A slice of smoked salmon (for protein, brain-boosting Omega-3 and not too much fat)
- Half a ripe avocado (good for blood circulation)
- A handful of baby spinach leaves (in memory tests rats that eat spinach learn and perform better)
- A few chopped walnuts (excellent brain food, with Omega-3 and Vitamin E to help keep your nervous system healthy).

Now

- Spread with a thin layer of cream cheese (there's calcium in cream cheese and butter, but cream cheese has less fat)
- Mix together with a little fresh lemon juice, olive oil, salt and pepper
- Spread this mixture on the bottom slice, slap on the top slice, cut it in half and there you have a very Clever Sandwich!

Make a meal of it

A Clever Lunchbox, could include:

- Your sandwich
- A small tub of blueberries or strawberries (full of magical 'flavonoids' that improve blood-flow to the brain, boosting your memory for up to five hours!)
- Two squares of dark chocolate (for more flavonoids)
- A bottle of fresh water – dehydration can give you a headache, and that's very bad for your brain.

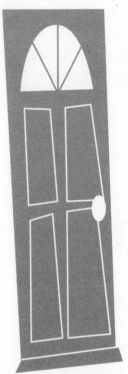

Sounds disgusting?

If you can't stand salmon, are allergic to walnuts, or think water's for wimps, you'll be pleased to know that scientists disagree about exactly how much good these foods will do for your brain. One thing's for certain though – to keep your brain healthy, you definitely need to eat healthily.

Brainbox – diet

A balanced diet can make a difference to your grades. In Canada, researchers gave 5,000 students a literacy test, and found that those on poor diets were much more likely to fail! A poor diet means too much fat (in foods like burgers and sausages), too many refined sugars (in cakes and sweets), and not enough fruit, veg and wholegrain foods (like brown bread). Remember, you need AT LEAST five portions of fruit and veg each day.

Oh, and never skip breakfast! If you're in a rush, grab a fruit smoothie for a long-lasting brain boost. If you've more time, make a plate of beans on toast or just some toast and Marmite.

Get clever with exercise

Experts around the world are concerned about the amount of exercise young people are getting, and worrying that it's not enough. They recommend at least an hour each day, not just to keep you healthy, but also to keep your brain buzzing.

You don't have to be great at sport for your brain to benefit — in fact one of the best forms of exercise is walking! Writers often go for a walk when they're stuck on a section, or need a new idea. Walking isn't a particularly strenuous activity, but it gets you breathing faster, so your heart pumps faster too, speeding up the blood-flow round your body. That helps you to think, learn, and remember better.

Running can be brilliant for your brain as well. Recent tests have shown that it actually encourages grey matter — the stuff in your brain, which helps you remember things — in the brain to grow. But they say your brain benefits most when you're running with your friends.

As for the best brain sport of all? Ping-Pong! Honestly, it is. Ping-Pong, or table tennis, is a fast-moving game, where you need to move and react as quickly as you can. It doesn't just get the blood pumping round your body, it also gets your brain working speedily. And the better you get, the faster you have to move, and the more you have to think up winning moves, so you are exercising your brain and your body loads.

There's plenty you can do if you think you're not exercising enough:

• If you don't walk to school already, now's the time to start. Live too far away? Ask to be dropped off a little way from the school, and walk the last half mile or so. Live too close? Why not set off early and call for friends who live a street or two away, so you can walk to school together.

• If you don't play active games at break time, encourage your classmates to have a game of tag with you. Is there a playing field at your school? See if you can get permission to play football, or run round the track with your friends at lunchtime.

• Get involved with after-school sports clubs. If there isn't a Ping-Pong club, you could always ask your school to start one.

Most important is to find a sport you enjoy, so exercising never feels like hard work.

But if you want to be a really clever sports person, then hard work is really what it's all about...

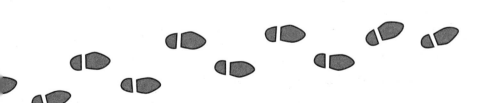

Famously clever: Tom Daley (born 1994)

When his dad asked him, at seven years old, whether he wanted to try diving at the local swimming pool, Tom Daley could have had no idea how much it was going to change his life. But soon after he first hit the water, it was obvious this little boy was going to do well. Three years later, he became British Under-18s Champion, at 13 he was European diving champion, and at 15 he became a world champion – making him the youngest ever British World Champion in any sport! In 2008, he was also one of the youngest ever competitors to take part in the Olympic Games and the first person ever to win BBC Young Sports Person of the Year three times.

Tom might have been a diving natural, but he still needed to work fantastically hard. And Tom wasn't even training full time because he still had to go to school! His rigorous schedule included one and a half hours' homework after school, followed by four hours of diving. Two mornings a week he'd put in a couple of hours' practice before school, with three hours on Saturday morning, followed by homework all afternoon. *Phew!*

With the distractions of his success, Tom could have been forgiven for flunking a few subjects, but instead — even though he had to sit some of his exams in China during the Beijing Olympics — he did brilliantly in his GCSEs, getting all As and A*s, and an A*, A and B in his A-Levels!

There are no footballer-style salaries in the world of diving, unfortunately, but Tom says he doesn't care, because nothing can beat the feeling that you're the best in the world.

Ten top tips for hassle-free homework

Ugh, homework. Hands up who likes it? Anyone? Didn't think so. You get it night after night, and then you're expected to do some in the holidays too. Research has shown though that it can help you to remember things you've learned in class, and build on new skills. And when it comes to exams, homework definitely improves your grades – though doing too much of it might not make a huge difference.

But cheer up, though you might not be able get out of doing it altogether, you can build homework in to your weekly routine and make it more enjoyable. Okay, so the words 'homework' and 'enjoyable' don't go together too well, but read on and then see what you think...

Getting down to it

1. Start by doing a bit of meditation (see p. 124), or listening to your favourite music (see p. 95) while you flick through the TV guide. Obviously, that won't answer any of your homework questions, but it will give you something to work towards. Find a few programmes you really want to watch, and be strict with yourself: complete one piece of homework for each programme, and do not allow yourself to watch TV until that work has been done.

If watching TV doesn't float your boat, promise yourself some time on a computer game, or think of something else to reward yourself with when you've finished. Your kind, generous parents might even offer a little pocket money for each piece of homework you complete, or you could suggest you work towards one big treat. They'll be so impressed with your organization they might actually say yes!

2. Find yourself a regular work space. It needs to be quiet – somewhere you can work without interruption. Gather everything you need before you start – pens, pencils, books, your computer, a comfort blanket – and settle down with a small dish of brain-boosting berries, and a mug of hot chocolate. Be sure to turn off the telly while you're working though!

3. If you have real trouble concentrating on what you're supposed to be doing it's probably because there are doors banging, phones ringing, dogs barking, mice scuttling under the floorboards or spiders noisily making webs. But try telling yourself to "Keep working!" a few times. That should help you to stay focused.

4. If you can't stop thinking about other stuff you have to do, put a separate piece of paper to one side of your work space. When your mind wanders from your homework, scribble down the spare thoughts on the blank sheet of paper to put it out of your mind until later, then turn back to your homework and **get on with it**.

Handling the homework

5. When it comes to the work itself, make yourself do the hardest piece first – yes, really! Once that's out of the way, you'll really feel you've achieved something.

6. If you get really stuck on something, try moving on to another piece of work for a while or taking a break and coming back to it later when you're refreshed.

7. Always read the instructions **really carefully!** Read them more than once, and if you're not sure what you're supposed to be doing, read them again, or get your mum or dad to read them out for you. Remember to check the date too. There's nothing worse than getting to the last question and realising that you've been doing last week's homework, you've been on the wrong page all along or you should have been multiplying, not dividing – *aaargh!*

8. Always, always allow time to read your work through before you finish. You could wait and do this the following day, but make sure you do it. It's amazing how many mistakes everyone makes without realizing. (See p. 76 for editorial tips.)

9. Once you're done, it's time to enjoy your reward. Sit back, relax and bask in your own brilliance at sorting out your homework.

10. After all your hard work, what's the one thing you absolutely have to do? **Remember to hand it in!**

143

BE CLEVER AT GEOGRAPHY

Watch travel programmes or disaster documentaries on TV, read articles about far-flung places, and you'll soon discover that geography is more interesting than you might have thought.

To get to know the world better, stick a nice big, detailed map on the wall of your bedroom, kitchen or even the bathroom. Try to find one that has a grid pattern on it.

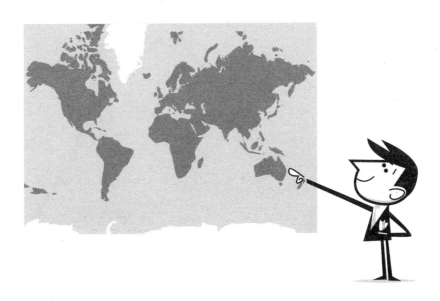

Every time you're near your map try looking for something new.

Knowing where places are in the world is a great way to sound clever, so it's worth spending a bit of time alone, just you and your map together...

Now think of lots of different reasons to look places up:
  • You went there on holiday
  • It's where your pet hamster/tarantula/armadillo comes from
  • Your great uncle Sergei lives there/your generous cousin Thelma went there on holiday
  • You like the sound of the name — Mongolia, Guam, Togo...
  • They're hosting the World Cup
  • It annoys the rest of your family when they have to wait ages for the loo.

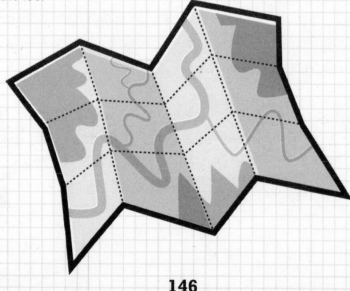

Capital countdown

There's no need to keep your map to yourself. Here's a fun way of sharing it with other people.

You will need

- A friend, brother, sister — parent even
- A map of the world
- A stopwatch
- A pen and paper.

Standing in front of the map, one person shouts out the name of a country, while the other tries desperately to find it on the map as fast as possible. When you've got the hang of that, make it a bit harder by moving on to capital cities (the more obscure the better: Ulaanbaatar, Ljubljana, Kuala Lumpur...). Use a stopwatch to work out how long it takes to find each country and note down your scores. When you finish, add up your scores. The winner is the one with the quickest time.

Now that you've got to know the map quite well, it's time to take in some facts. These are a few things that all good geographers should know...

Brainbox – the world

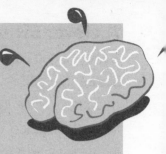

According to the United Nations, the world's population hit SEVEN BILLION on 31st October 2011. (See p. 90 to work out just how many that is.)

One hundred years ago it was just 1,750,000,000 (fewer than two billion!). We hit four billion in 1974.

By 2050, if the population keeps growing at the same rate, there'll be well over nine billion people on the planet!

A clever bit of geography

Is there a grid pattern on your map? This is really handy for finding places. The grid lines are called 'meridians'. The 'lines of latitude' run across – the latitude line marked '0' is the equator – and the 'lines of longitude' run up and down – the longitude line marked '0' is the Greenwich meridian, shown here in this close-up. Wherever the lines end, you'll see a number. You can use these numbers to locate places – or to put it cleverly, 'find the co-ordinates' of a place.

Greenwich meridian

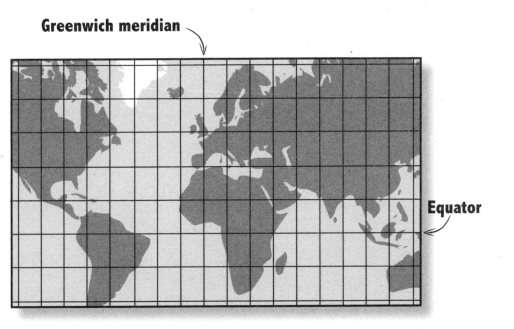

Equator

Now, can you find Tokyo on your world map using just these lines and numbers? The co-ordinates for Tokyo are, 35.68° North and 139.77° East, but you can just say 36°N and 140°E.

Look to the left, or east of your map above the equator, and find the line that is labelled '30°N'. Then run your finger a little way above the line to find 36°N. Put a finger from your left hand on this point.

Now look at the top, or north, of your map and find the line that says either '135°' or '140°', depending on how your map is labelled. Put a finger from your right hand here. Now slowly move each finger along its line, until they meet in the middle. You should now have both fingers roughly on Tokyo.

Have a go at playing Capital Countdown again. This time, don't say the name of the city – give the co-ordinates instead!

Fantastic geography facts

Try finding co-ordinates for some of the places mentioned in these facts...

The earth is 70% water, and 97% of that is sea water. Only 3% is fresh water, which humans and animals can drink.

There are five oceans. From the largest to the smallest: Pacific, Atlantic, Indian, Southern, Arctic.

The Pacific Ocean touches four continents, and 25,000 islands! Pacific means 'peaceful', but there's some unsettling stuff going on underneath its waves.

75% of the world's volcanoes are found in the Pacific Ocean, and 80% of the world's largest earth tremors happen here too, in a band known as the Pacific Ring of Fire.

The Pacific Ocean is around 4 kilometres deep. But trenches in the Pacific are much deeper. The bottom of the Mariana Trench, the deepest point on earth, is 11 kilometres below the surface of the water. The co-ordinates are roughly 11°N and 142°E.

Brain Box – Mariana Trench

In 1960, Don Walsh and Jacques Piccard
were the first people to go to the bottom
of the Mariana Trench. They travelled in a
specially designed submersible vessel, called
Trieste. The journey down took nearly five hours and they
only stopped at the bottom for 20 minutes. They couldn't see
much though because the vessel had disturbed the ground
and made the water all murky!

The Nile is the longest river in the world, stretching a fantastic 6,650 kilometres from Burundi, south of the equator, through ten countries, and out through Egypt, into the Mediterranean Sea.

The White Nile and the Blue Nile are two 'tributary' rivers, which flow into the Nile.

On average the Nile is 2.8 kilometres wide, stretching to a whopping 7.5 kilometres at its widest point and about 8-11 metres deep.

The highest mountain in the world is Everest – named after geographer, George Everest. It's part of the Himalayan mountain range and sits between two countries, Tibet and Nepal. In Tibet it's called 'Chomolungma', and in Nepal, it's 'Sagamartha'.

Everest is a whopping 8,848 metres high, and it's growing! It's reckoned the mountain is gaining around 1 centimetre in height each year! You can find it on the map at roughly 28°N, 87°E.

Brain Box — Everest
The first people to climb Everest were Edmund Hillary, from New Zealand, and Tenzing Norgay, from Nepal. They reached the top in 1953. Since then hundreds of people have climbed the mountain — not that it's an easy climb. People die on the mountain every year because of avalanches, or they run out of oxygen. It's thought that there are at least 120 dead bodies lying frozen on the mountainside.

There's a lot to search out on a map of the world, so it's sometimes good to try looking at a smaller area. Your country, or local area are almost certainly interesting too, so why not stick up maps of these places on your walls and get clever on a local level?

No matter how much you stare at that map, though, you'll probably never get to know the world quite as well as one brave sailor...

Famously clever: Dame Ellen MacArthur (born 1976)

Ellen MacArthur was only four years old when she first went out in her auntie's boat, but from that day onwards, she constantly read books and magazines about boats. Even though she lived in Derbyshire, nowhere near the sea, Ellen saved up her dinner money and bought her very own dinghy, which she kept in her bedroom.

By 17, she had her own sailing boat, and at 18, she sailed it around Britain, becoming Young Sailor of the Year in 1995.

In 2000, Ellen was only 24 but entered the toughest sailing race there is — the Vendée Globe. Contestants have to sail their boat around the world, on their own, without stopping!

No one had heard of Ellen before the race, but by the end, everyone was talking about her. She didn't win, but did come second AND she smashed two world records: the youngest person ever to sail non-stop around the world and the fastest woman ever to sail non-stop around the world!

In 2005, Ellen became the fastest person ever to sail on her own, non-stop around the world. In 1969, a man named Robin Knox-Johnson had set the first ever record for the 27,000-mile journey at 312 days. Ellen did it in 71 days, 14 hours, 18 minutes and 33 seconds!

So just what did Ellen have to battle with on that record-breaking trip? Well, she had to climb the 98-foot mast in howling winds to fix the mainsail — twice, eating nothing but freeze-dried food, go without a single decent night's sleep and do all of it completely on her own.

Ellen got to know the planet better than most while she was sailing around it. She has now given up sailing competitively and instead is working on the biggest challenge of all: finding a way to save it!

Have you got square eyes?

Has anyone ever said to you: "If you sit in front of that screen much longer you'll get square eyes"? Are you guilty of too much screen time? Try this quiz to find out.

1. After a hard day at school do you:

a) Walk home listening to music then sit in front of the TV, computer or games console moving only to accept drinks and dinner, until you fall asleep?

b) Rush straight to your desk and get on with your homework, read a big textbook and try a few experiments before tea?

c) Stay at school for athletics club, then head for home and the telly/computer/games console. Get your homework done, have tea, then watch an hour of TV, and squeeze in a bit of social networking before bed?

2. When it comes to watching TV programmes do you:

a) Just switch on and start watching – not caring if you see the same cartoons a zillion times over?

b) Only watch programmes on the Discovery Channel, or if they're linked to the Open University?

c) Check out the guide and feel spoilt for choice, from cartoons to cookery, documentaries to historical dramas, you like the variety TV has to offer?

3. When a TV programme finishes you:

a) Can hardly remember anything about it, you've just let it wash over you?

b) Have filled an A4 fine-lined jotter with notes about everything, from the facts included, to ideas for your own TV shows?

c) Decide whether or not you liked the programme and remember the best bits so you can chat to your mates about them?

4. You use computers for:

a) Games, games and more games, the more guns and shooting the better.

b) Research purposes and homework only – though maybe you have your own blog?

c) Research and homework, games and social networking; you like experimenting and playing around with what the computer can do too?

Be honest now. Which type describes you best? Are you more of an a), b) or c)? Let's find out how clever you screen habits are:

Mostly **A**s: You are well over the recommended one to two hours of screen time a day … along with loads of other British five to 16 year olds (who watch an average of SIX hours a day!). Trouble is, sitting around, not exercising, using your brain, or meeting up with friends can mean you damage your health, have problems with your schoolwork and even change the way you act.

Mostly **B**s: You may be bordering on brilliant, with teacher-pleasing TV and homework habits, but maybe you should find more balance? Getting good grades is great, but you need a bit of fun too. Go outside whenever you can, run around and have a laugh with a few friends and maybe try watching a cartoon or two.

Mostly **C**s: You seem to have the balance just about right. You enjoy some screen time, but you also have plenty of other stuff going on. When you watch TV you're choosing your programmes carefully and remembering to keep your brain awake. Well done! But there's still more you can do. Read on to find out...

How to use screens cleverly

- Stick with 1-2 hours of screen time a day, then play outside, draw, read books ... try some activities from this book.
- Don't just watch whatever happens to be on TV, use the guide and choose your programmes carefully.
- Try different programmes: the news helps to keep you informed, even cookery programmes can be fun to watch.
- If you watch a drama, comedy or movies on TV, ask yourself questions about it, and think about how it's filmed.
- If you have to watch adverts, think about what the makers want you to do.
- Try setting yourself a time limit for computer games – have a day or two a week when you don't play at all.
- Try to choose games that could help with your homework.
- Use the computer to get creative – play around with photos, make movies or cards for your friends.

If you manage to do even a few of these then you'll definitely be on your way to being really clever!

BE CLEVER
AT HISTORY

A world before you is hard to imagine isn't it? But amazingly enough, people just like you – *homo sapiens* – have been living on the planet for 200,000 years, and the species had been evolving for 3 million years before that. People have always needed to eat, work, protect and entertain themselves, and actually it can be surprisingly interesting finding out about the different ways they've done it.

Your own family history can be a really interesting starting point — maybe:

- Your dad's great uncle Tarquin travel to Outer Mongolia on a penny farthing
- Your great-great Aunt Betty was evacuated to America during the Second World War
- Your Granny is always talking about how she always used to eat real food and how much better life used to be.

Next time Gran starts reminiscing, give her a bit of encouragement. Ask a few questions. There's a term for what she has to tell you — it's called 'living history'. Your Gran has experiences of things in the past that you might be glad to know about in the future.

The best way to get clever about history is by getting involved in it. Asking questions is an excellent way to start because history is full of incredible stories. Your own family probably has a few — and if you don't know any, ask. But while you might be able to trace your family back one or maybe even two hundred years, there's another family tree that's so well recorded it goes back a thousand years! It belongs to the British royal family and you'll be shocked and appalled at what they got up to...

Remember your kings and queens

If you can memorize this rhyme, you'll know the order of all the kings and queens of England from William the Conqueror right through to Queen Elizabeth II, and that has got to make you look clever! Knowing the royal family tree can be a useful way of getting to grips with what was happening in Britain over the last nine hundred years too.

Willie, Willie, Henry, Steve
Henry, Rich, John, Henry Three
Edward One, Two, Three, Rich Two
Henry Four, Five, Six, then who?
Eds Four Five, then Rich the Bad[1]
Two more Henrys, Ed — dead lad[2]
Mary, Liz One, James the Vain[3],
Charles, pause[4], Charles, then James again.
William and Mary, Anne o'Gloria[5]
Georges Four, Will and Victoria
Edward Seven, Georgie Five
Edward, George and Liz (alive)

Fights, plots, beheadings, jealousies
… it all happened with this lot in power.
Read on to find out about a few of them —
the facts match up with the little numbers
in the rhyme…

1. Richard III is called Rich the Bad, because at the beginning of his reign, in 1483, his two nephews, Edward and Richard – princes who he was supposed to be protecting – mysteriously disappeared from the Tower of London. Nobody knows whodunnit, but 'Bad' King Rich got the blame.

2. Edward VI was Henry VIII's only son. He was a sickly child, but quite clever (and very well educated). He was only nine when his dad died in 1547, and by 15, he himself was a dead lad. The next bottom to hit the throne is not recorded in this rhyme – it was kicked off again nine days later by Ed's big sister, 'Bloody' Mary. That bottom belonged to Ed's cousin Lady Jane Grey – she was just sixteen when she got her head chopped off.

3. King James I of England and Ireland was also James VI of Scotland and after his arrival in England, from 1603 onwards, the three countries shared the same monarch. He came straight after Elizabeth I, who had, rather nastily, chopped off his mum's head a few years earlier.

James was probably called 'vain' because early historians reckoned he didn't know as much as he liked to think he knew about world affairs. However, some of today's historians say he was the most well-read royal that Britain has ever had.

4. The reason for the 'pause' here is that, shockingly, Britain didn't have a king or queen for a while. A civil war started in 1642, which divided the English people between supporting Parliament — the Roundheads — or the King — the Cavaliers. King Charles I ended up getting the chop, and ordinary, non-royal, Oliver Cromwell took his place as 'Lord Protector of England, Scotland and Ireland'. Cromwell died in 1658, but three years later, his body was dug up, hanged, beheaded, and his head put on public display. Revolting! By this time though, Charles's son — also Charles — had returned from France, where he'd been in exile, and had become King himself.

5. Queen Anne was the little sister of Queen Mary, and Mary ruled with her Dutch husband, William III. The pair had got rid of James II — Mary and Anne's Catholic dad — so they could grab the throne back for the Protestants and stop Mary's baby brother inheriting the crown. The trouble kicked off in 1688, and was known as the Glorious Revolution! Anne took over once Mary and William had died, but she'd never have been queen if the Glorious Revolution hadn't happened. That's what the 'Anne O'Gloria' bit in the rhyme means.

Dates to remember

Today you can study the history of just about anything, but people will always be impressed if you can drop a few dates into a conversation. It's a good idea to know roughly what you're talking about though. So before you start to 'date-drop', swat up on some background info, then see if you can make it rhyme...

The date: AD* 79

What you need to know:
The wealthy city of Pompeii was minding its own business on 24th August AD 79, when nearby volcano, Vesuvius, decided to erupt. Thousands fled the city, but around 2,000 stayed. Gases blasted from the volcano and poisoned all those left behind. Then the city disappeared under layers of volcanic ash, and everyone forgot where it had been!

* AD is short for *anno Domini*, meaning 'in the year of our Lord'. According to the Western date system, Jesus was born in the year 0. Dates before 0 are counted backwards, and have BC (before Christ) after them. Dates after 0 are counted forwards and can have AD in front of them.

We know quite a lot about what happened because:

1. A boy called Pliny, watched the eruption from 20 miles away and wrote about it.

2. Over 1,500 years after the event, the site was discovered. Some of the buildings were a bit beaten up, but otherwise, everything was exactly as it had been when the lava landed — except the bodies of the dead had turned to stone. It wasn't much fun for the petrified bodies, but historians were ecstatic — that's one way we know so much about what life was like nearly 2,000 years ago.

How to remember it:

When Vesuvius flowed with lava, in AD 79,
Pompeii was preserved to the end of time.

The date: 1066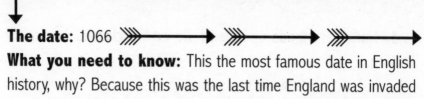

What you need to know: This the most famous date in English history, why? Because this was the last time England was invaded and conquered – over 900 years ago! The Normans took power, and French became the language of posh people. It was a busy year and you could fill a whole book with everything that happened, but these are the main highlights:

1. Edward the Confessor was king, but he died.

2. Harold, Earl of Wessex, grabbed the crown and became the new king.

3. William the Conqueror – also known as the Duke of Normandy – claimed he should be king.

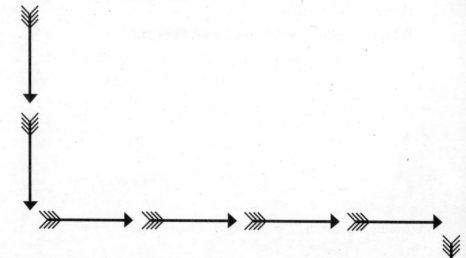

4. Harald Hardrada — King of Norway — claimed he should be king.

5. Harald invaded in the north, but Harold (the Wessex one) fought him off. Harald died, and Harold hurried south.

6. William invaded. Harold got there late. William conquered and King Harold was killed.

William and Harold fought at Hastings. The battle only lasted a day, but it's been remembered ever after, partly because of the Bayeux Tapestry that is on display in France, which tells its story — including how Harold was shot in the eye with an arrow — *ouch!*

➤ How to remember it:
Battle of Hastings, ten sixty-six
Will got Harold* in the eye with a pointy stick.

* It probably wasn't actually William who shot Harold, but it works for the rhyme.

The date: 1348

What you need to know: The Black Death was a terrifying plague that swept from Asia, along all the trade routes, to Europe. It arrived in England in 1348, and hurried from town to town, leaving a terrifying trail of destruction. It's thought over one third of the population of Europe died from the Black Death.

Symptoms included lumps under the arms and on the legs, neck and groin, fever and sickness. Once you'd got it, you didn't last more than a couple of days!

Scientists today are still trying to find out exactly what caused the plague, but rats have generally taken the blame. Although to be fair, the fleas that hitched a lift on their fur were probably the guilty ones.

People of the time didn't help themselves — they tipped the contents of their chamber pots out on to the streets below, where animals wandered about freely. Water was generally filthy too — ideal conditions for a deadly disease to spread.

How to remember it:
Black Death hit the Brits in thirteen forty-eight
Black boils, sweats and sickness — *ew!* A grisly fate.

The date: 1492

What you need to know: Christopher Columbus wasn't even looking for a new country when he set sail from Spain and accidentally bumped into America – The Bahamas to be precise – on October 12, 1492. He was searching for a route to China and thought he'd arrived in India. (That's why he called the Native Americans 'Indians'.)

People used to say that Christopher Columbus 'discovered' America, but of course, the Native Americans had already been living there for thousands of years! Even the Vikings had visited already. But it was only after Columbus arrived that Europeans began to think about living on the new continent. And that was very bad news for the Native Americans. Millions died horrible deaths from the diseases, war and slavery that the Europeans brought with them.

How to remember it:

In fourteen hundred and ninety-two,
Columbus sailed the ocean blue.

The date: 1859

What you need to know: This was the year that Charles Darwin published his book, *On the Origin of Species*. He'd been so nervous about the publication that he'd waited twenty years! Why? Because the ideas inside the book suggested that people might be just another type of animal and that they might even have evolved from apes! Up until then, people had believed the story from the Bible – that God had taken six days to make the world and everything in it. People were horrified – this changed everything they believed in. Even so, they couldn't wait to get their hands on the book. By 1901, it had sold over 100,000 copies!

How to remember it:

Origin of Species, eighteen fifty-nine
Darwin added apes to the human timeline.

DIY dates

You could do a bit of research yourself and see if you can find a few good dates to remember. Try these for starters. Look up the dates and see if you can work out the event they relate to. Read up about it, and think about a rhyme to make sure you never forget what happened on this date.

1314 a Scottish battle

1452 a ground-breaking book

1605 a plan uncovered

1666 a disaster in London

1799 a surprising stone

1815 a famous battle

1912 a dreadful disaster

1914-1918 a terrible war

1939-1945 another terrible war

1963 the death of a president

2001 a treacherous attack.

Famously clever: Gertrude Bell (1868-1926)

Gertrude Bell grew up northeast England in a wealthy family. She was home-schooled at first but later went off to school in London, where her history teachers quickly realized her brilliance and suggested she should try for Oxford University.

In 1886, Gertrude went to Lady Margaret Hall at Oxford University to study history and she was the first woman who graduated with a first-class degree in Modern History, which is the top grade you can get.

Victorian England didn't have much to offer clever women like Gertrude and, ever searching for adventure, she taught herself Persian and took herself off to Persia — now Iran in the Middle East — and wrote a book about the country. She later learned Arabic, taught herself Archaeology and even took up mountaineering. She famously perched on a cliff-face for over 50 hours, as a blizzard swept over her expedition. She even got involved in Middle Eastern politics and completed two round-the-world trips!

Gertrude was one History graduate who, through exploration, archaeology and languages, went on to make history herself.

BE CLEVER AT SCIENCE

If you want to be clever at science, you need to be ace at asking questions. Good scientists are very curious and they like to show that other people's ideas are wrong or make them even better by doing their own experiments. And that's why science is so exciting, because it's always changing.

To get cleverer at science, keep a notebook with you at all times, so you can write down your questions, ideas and thoughts. The white coat is optional, but learning a bit of scientific language is pretty much essential. Scientists may not try to baffle people on purpose, but they do have a habit of using really long words when short ones would do.

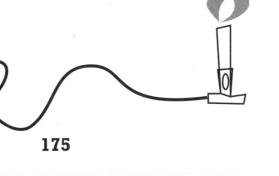

Speak like a scientist

Analysis: Scientists love to analyse, or 'look closely' at things — preferably with a microscope or even a telescope.

Conclusion: This comes at the end of an experiment and explains why you did the test in the first place and what you found out.

Data: The information or results found from doing an experiment.

Fair test: Any small change you make to an experiment you do should be part of a fair test — only one thing should change.

Generate: The scientific word for 'make'.

Hypothesis: This is a statement of 'fact' that hasn't yet been proved to be true or false — you would hope to prove in your experiment.

Magnitude: Another way of saying how big something is.

Norm: It's just a shortened version of 'normal'.

Observations: The things you notice and jot down in your notebook.

Prediction: At the start of an experiment, the scientist tries guessing, or working out, what the result might be.

Quantifiable: Whether you can work out how much something weighs, how big it is, or measure it.

Theory: An idea, or series of ideas, that explains something that happens, but hasn't been proved to be true or false.

Variable: Something that has been changed from the 'norm' in an experiment to see what effect it has.

A serious science experiment ...
... with a sensational result!

To get an idea of how scientists work, have a go at this experiment. It's been done before, but try it out just for fun. Then you can try to learn something new from it.

You will need

- Small canisters with tight-fitting, snap-on lids or plastic tubes and push-on lids (not screw-tops!)
- Alka Seltzer tablets (or other effervescent, or fizzy, tablets)
- Lots of outside space well away from other people, animals or delicate ornaments
- A lab coat – or better still, a plastic raincoat ... and umbrella ... and goggles
- Permission, and some help from an adult.

What to do

1. Add water to the canister/tube, so it is about a quarter full (hold this in one hand).

2. Pop an Alka Seltzer tablet inside the lid (hold this in the other hand).

3. Rush outside.

4. Push the lid quickly and firmly onto the canister, so the water and the tablet start to mix. Turn the canister upside down and stand well back (but not so far that you can't still see the canister).

5. Wait, and wait, and wait … just as you think nothing's going to happen, something should happen…

If all goes predictably, and you didn't get showered with froth, you'll have wondered how on earth that little capsule was projected right over your garden shed! But why?

Well, the tablets contain sodium bicarbonate – used in baking to help cakes rise – and citric acid, which probably came from lemon juice. When these two ingredients are mixed with water, they have a chemical reaction that creates the gases carbon dioxide and sodium citrate. The reaction generates heat, and the heat increases the pressure of the gas. The pressure builds and builds until the canister and the lid are blown apart.

How to conduct a proper experiment

If you want to get clever with this experiment, and do it scientifically, you'll need to make a few changes. Do the experiment again, but this time...

You will also need

- A notebook
- A pencil
- A stopwatch or timer
- A measuring jug with millimetres marked.

Do the experiment as before, but remember to:

- Note down exactly how much water you put in the canister.
- Start the timer as soon as you place the canister on the ground.
- Stop the timer as soon as the canister flies off.
- Note down how long it took for the canister and lid to pop apart.
- Note down roughly how high you think the canister has flown.

It's difficult to measure exactly, so maybe compare its flight to the height of an object or series of objects, like a nearby tree, or wall.

This is your controlled experiment. The data you get from the experiment will provide a norm for you to work from.

Now you can try different versions of the experiment. But, in order to make sure you are carrying out a fair test you must keep all details exactly the same, except for ONE variable.

You could try changing

• The liquid you put in the canister – for hot water, a fizzy drink, fruit juice, vinegar– and keep the amount exactly the same

• The amount of liquid you put in the canister

• How much of the tablet you put in – try halving it, or putting in two tablets

• The type of tablet you use. Try a vitamin C tablet, or any other effervescing tablet.

Before you start any new experiments, though, remember to jot down a prediction of what you think will happen.

How to write up your experiment

It's easy! You've got your notes, so all you need to do now is write up your experiment. Use the headings below and remember to sprinkle your report with plenty of science speak…

- Experiment title
- Record your prediction — what you think will happen
- List your equipment — what you used
- Explain your method — say what you did
- Record your results — what actually happened
- Draw a conclusion — say why you think it happened.

Your research paper will look especially scientific if you include a graph or two filled in with your fascinating data. You could show the length of time it takes the lids to pop off the canisters, compared to how much water you put in.

But how do scientists use all their findings? Well, when they discover something interesting, they will probably write a paper about it in the hope of getting it published in a science journal. Then other scientists might try out their experiment to see if they can build on the idea. Scientists are pretty good at sharing their findings, it's something they've been doing for a very long time…

Famously clever: Galileo Galilei (1564-1642)

Galileo was born in Italy in 1564, and started off studying medicine, but he soon changed his mind and switched to mathematics. It's a good thing he did because there's lots we might not know, and many inventions we wouldn't have without Galileo.

Galileo built the first water pump and in 1609 he built one of the world's first telescopes. It was so good that he discovered sunspots on the sun, the four largest moons orbiting Jupiter and the mountains and valleys on the surface of the moon. He also made important discoveries about gravity that Sir Isaac Newton later improved on (see p. 184).

(see p. 184).

For years, people had thought that heavier objects fall faster than lighter objects, but Galileo proved this theory wrong. He said that if you drop two objects in a vacuum (somewhere with no air) they will fall at the same speed. Not everyone thought Galileo was so clever though – the church didn't like his theories and put him under house arrest (like being in jail in your own home) in 1633, for the rest of his life!

But Galileo's findings lived on after he had died, and had a huge impact on future scientists…

Famously clever: Sir Isaac Newton (1642-1727)

When Isaac went to school, he wasn't considered very bright, but he studied hard and in the end, did well. In 1661, he went to Cambridge University, where he became interested in maths and science. Isaac did an awful lot of thinking about gravity, and used Galileo's findings to help work out his three laws of motion:

1. An object will stay still, or continue moving in a straight line, unless it is affected by another object, or force.

2. Heavier objects need more energy to speed up or slow down.

3. When one object pushes against another object, the other object pushes back just as hard.

Isaac worked out the rules to help understand how the stars and planets move, and people were pretty pleased with his theories. In fact, they didn't really bother to question them until over 200 years later, when Einstein published his General Theory of Relativity (see p. 24).

Isaac famously said: "If I have seen further it is only by standing on the shoulders of Giants" – that is, each new discovery can only happen by building on the work of other scientists. Perhaps he was thinking about the scientists who had gone before him, but maybe he wondered too about those who were still to come…

Famously clever: Stephen Hawking (born 1942)

Stephen Hawking was born in Oxford on 8th January 1942, exactly 300 years after Galileo's death. He is probably the most famous living physicist.

Stephen went to University College at Oxford University, where his dad also studied. He didn't work very hard, but left with the highest grade – a first-class degree in Physics. He then went to study for a PhD in Cosmology at Cambridge University. But at 21, doctors told him he had motor neurone disease and that his muscles would gradually waste away. They said he would be dead in three to five years.

Stephen found after a while that he couldn't write. By the 1970s, he was in a wheelchair, and by the early 1980s, his speech was almost impossible to understand. He was still very much alive though. Stephen got a computerized system for his speech in 1986. Today he can only operate it by twitching his cheek. Amazingly, Stephen celebrated his seventieth birthday in 2012!

Stephen has focused his studies on black holes, but he has also written three children's books, a bestselling book called *A Brief History of Time* and appeared in *The Simpsons*. He has received lots awards and was the Lucasian Professor of Mathematics from 1979 until 2009, a job previously held by Sir Isaac Newton – *wow!* One thing he hasn't done yet that he really wants to do is to go into space.

The ups and downs of being a total genius

Wouldn't it be brilliant if you were... well, brilliant? If you were a genius, life would be so much easier. Wouldn't it?

The ups

• School work would be *eeeeasy*, with no need to try to hard in class, you'd breeze through the day.

• You could get your homework done on the walk home from school and have time to watch wall-to-wall cartoons all evening.

• You'd probably be teacher's pet.

• Other pupils would look up to you and you'd find you were their favourite too – for explaining tricky stuff to them and helping them with their homework.

• Exams, tests? Huh, those wouldn't get in your way. With just a quick flick through the books at breakfast you'd whizz through each paper in a few short minutes.

Of course, that's what we all think it might be like to be a genius, but if you're not getting A*s every week, don't worry...

The downs

• You might take no time over homework, but then you'd love to study anyway! That's one of the ways you got to be so clever.

• Genius isn't always recognized straightaway (remember what they said about Albert Einstein – see p. 23), and teachers often don't like having a pupil in the class who is cleverer than them.

• Your friends would constantly nag you to help them with their homework and it's no fun doing the same work twice!

• Nobody wants to finished an exam paper in five seconds flat, and get every question right — then you'd be sat there bored for ages!

• If you're studying all the time then you won't have time to go out and play with your friends, watch TV or get the high score on computer games.

So what do you think? Still fancy being a genius? Well, if you do you don't have to have brilliant parents, or get straight As all the time at school. Your brilliance might not even be noticed for another 20 years — and it may have nothing to do with the subjects you've learned at school.

Some people think genius is handed out before you're born, but recent research says that's not true, it agrees with Dr Suzuki's ideas (see p. 106). A really good teacher can help enormously, but it seems that to develop a serious gift for music, sport, art, science, maths ... takes practice. A specific amount of practice, actually: at least 10,000 hours over ten long years to be precise. That's nearly three hours a day every day! Could you abandon the games console, avoid chatting online, and stop the regular kick-around in the park for that?

If that doesn't sound like much fun to you, then stop worrying about being brilliant. Don't even worry about how clever everyone else is compared to you. Instead, keep working hard, remember everyone is clever in different ways and it's not always subjects you study at school that will be your cleverest. Eat clever sandwiches, do brain exercises, try boosting your memory, your writing, your literacy, but most of all, look for something you love to do — and, well, work at it. Working hard at something you love really isn't a chore, and it can have fantastic results.

Every brain can do incredible things, so there's plenty inside that skull of yours to play around with. You might not be a total genius yet, but you definitely can work towards fantastic results.